Politactics

Political Conversations
from Everyday Analysis

Politactics

Political Conversations
from Everyday Analysis

EDA Collective
Edited by Alfie Bown and Daniel Bristow

Winchester, UK
Washington, USA

First published by Zero Books, 2016
Zero Books is an imprint of John Hunt Publishing Ltd., Laurel House, Station Approach,
Alresford, Hants, SO24 9JH, UK
office1@jhpbooks.net
www.johnhuntpublishing.com
www.zero-books.net

For distributor details and how to order please visit the 'Ordering' section on our website.

Text copyright: EDA Collective 2015

ISBN: 978 1 78535 436 6
Library of Congress Control Number: 2016934230

A CIP catalogue record for this book is available from the British Library.

Design: Stuart Davies

Printed in the USA by Edwards Brothers Malloy

We operate a distinctive and ethical publishing philosophy in all
areas of our business, from our global network of authors to
production and worldwide distribution.

CONTENTS

1

Prologue: *Politactics*

i)

This third, short volume of Everyday Analysis writings aims to address and respond primarily to events in the field of politics, a central and perennial theme in our work. It looks to assess the unconscious *politactics* employed by the powers that are, and to also *politactically* challenge, and even change, them. It re-presents certain articles that have appeared on our online publications that have focused on political issues and writes 'around' them. Thus, the articles excerpted within these pages we approach in certain respects as 'case studies', which centrifugally spawn other bodies of text and discussion that draw on their themes and deliberate on their consequences. The title chosen for this book, *Politactics*, aims to achieve a couple of things. First, in part, to show up the type of accusatory riposte that so tirelessly gets wheeled out in response to criticism of political agendas: that of the 'but what's the alternative?', 'how would you do it better?', and 'if it's so bad, why don't you change it?'s. The type of political criticism in question is most often that being made by the Left and these responses often come from a Right who are either in power, and would wish to bar any access to any resources with which an alternative could be attempted to be implemented, or who support this Power and want either to 'rubbish' the opposition by mocking their relative impotence (that is, rather, often *disenablement*) or fully subscribe to a certain *realism* – 'capitalist realism', as Mark Fisher adroitly calls it – the ideological underpinning of which is so tightly sewn up as to make its fantasy appear the only possible reality in town... or both.[1] Secondly, however, the title is also chosen for the reason that we nonetheless do make some attempts within these pages – as far as is possible – to lay out certain forms of tactical response, on which to base a politics going forward, and enough separate attempts to warrant the modification on the word, too, to *polytactics*.

In some academic circles it has become commonplace to compare politics with a capital 'P' to politics with a small 'p'. This gesture is intended to indicate that while there is a subject called 'Politics' (with a big 'P'), which designates a certain kind of discussion or act, in fact everything that we do or say is or at least should be 'political' (with its small 'p'). The latter point has validity insofar as it forces us to recognise that all actions and comments are grounded in and caused by political conditions and that all actions and comments have political effects. Realising this means realising that there are no innocent and apolitical acts, and that everything needs to be interrogated. However, this primarily 'academic' idea has often become little more than a justification for academic thought and discussion not to engage with what it dismisses as 'Politics', with a capital 'P'. Academics may congratulate themselves on making 'political' difference whilst 'Politics' charges on as powerfully as ever. The end result may be that 'Politics' continues to do what it wants and the academia continues to do what it enjoys, whilst pretending to 'political' importance. In the end, 'Politics' (with a capital 'P') will likely cut academic funding before academia realises that it has been shooting itself in the foot in this respect for decades. Thus, the name of this book, *Politactics*, also looks to respond to this problem and to cut a path across the gap between the small 'p' and the capital 'P' so that 'Politics' is forced into conversation with not only academia, but with other modes of discourse as well. This book is therefore a collection of 'political' articles on the subject of 'Politics'.

Whereas previously we've written on the mechanism of a political elite selling the story to its public that: 'you don't have to concern yourselves with nasty politics… leave that whole funny business to us politicians', this contrivance sometimes goes further.[2] There are those who will criticise non-politicians for involving themselves with – or in – politics at all. One example is the constant questioning of why Owen Jones doesn't/won't become an MP (mirrored on its other side with the sentiment: 'he'll no doubt sell out and become an MP…').[3] It is this that we also attack 'politactically', by emphasising what should be the obvious: one doesn't *have* to be a politician to think about, comment on, try to alter the course of, agitate and advocate on behalf of or for changes to, be active or an activist about, Politics (with that big 'P'; and we hope this is where we may finally collapse the small one into the big).

These ruminations, however, also lead us to a classificatory problem at the heart of this book. That is, how to decide which of the many political articles from our contributors could or should be counted as articles on Politics. In the end, this may be an impossible problem to overcome. If one insists on strict criteria (only counting the articles that directly discuss politicians, governmental policy, or things that existing mainstream media discusses under the heading of 'Politics') then one risks prolifer-ating and entrenching the limits and restrictions that characterise our current political system, allowing politics to remain a closed language, which excludes and ignores other types of language and topics of discussion. On the other hand, if we were to follow the university in simply seeing everything as political, the book would quickly become something too far removed from Politics to make any impact in the field, falling into the same trap that the academia often has. In order to attempt to make as big an imprint on Politics as a small book through a left-wing press possibly can, we have in general kept close to what is generally considered Political discussion. To push the boundaries of existing political discourse we have tried to write at the limits of this language, on the edges of what is called Politics, bringing in other things with which politics is clearly and closely bound. The aim: to blur the distinction between politics and Politics, a distinction that has allowed Politics to survive for so long under-interrogated.

ii)

A major theme of this edition is reflected in a passage taken from Theodor Adorno's *Minima Moralia* concerning the objective/subjective divide and the mixing-up of this divide's terms:

> The notions of subjective and objective have been completely reversed. Objective means the non-controversial aspect of things, their unquestioned impression, the façade made up of classified data, that is, the subjective; and they call subjective anything which breaches that façade, engages the specific experience of a matter, casts off all ready-made judgements and substitutes relatedness to the object for the majority consensus of those who do not even look at it, let alone think about it – that is, the objective.[4]

In our analyses of media we suggest how it is often the case that a news organisation will move a thoroughly subjective perspective into the place or position of 'objectivity'. For example, terrestrial television channels' news stories detailing human(itarian) crises often cannot avoid discussion of the effect that these have on the markets, as if costs to capitalism objectively outweigh costs to humanity. The financialisation of everyday life is everywhere in the media; a great majority of tabloid headlines include some monetary figure that we're meant to assume is a cost somehow to ourselves. Another example comes in the form of a petition that calls for the BBC to refer to David Cameron as 'the right-wing Prime Minister' in response to their labelling Jeremy Corbyn 'the left-wing Labour leader' at every mention.[5] Whilst its observation is a ticklish one its point is a serious one: how better to manufacture a version of 'objectivity' than to erase every epithet for a certain personage, party or class, and thus present it as a norm to which everything else that gets any precautionary label is an exception? Should this get taken as the norm by readers, listeners and viewers, this will lead to the version of the 'objective' that Adorno alludes to, where things become 'non-controversial' and their 'impression' goes 'unquestioned'; that is, become subjectively accepted, as reality itself (hence this really being the realm of the 'subjective'). In contradistinction, what becomes known as the 'subjective' is 'anything which breaches that façade, engages the specific experience of a matter, casts off all ready-made judgements and substitutes relatedness to the object for the majority consensus of those who do not even look at it, let alone think about it'. That is, if, presented with an object, one does not toe the populist line or offer the stock consensus-reality response, this is seen, even vilified, as a purely *subjective* intervention; an anomaly, or perversion of the objective. However, surely, a 'relatedness to the object' must rather accord with objectivity: it is objective – when confronted with an object – to think about, engage with,'cast of all ready-made judgements' about, and analyse the specificity of, that object.

But to swap these modes of relations and social bonds for one another is in effect to *pathologise* thinking for the public consciousness as a subjective abnormality, rather than to see it (or allow it to be seen), democratically, as an objective right, utilisable by all those bestowed with the faculties that facilitate thinking. In his *Proust and Signs*, Gilles Deleuze argues that 'objectivity can no longer exist except in the work of art' – that is, in the creative work, or act – and goes on to state that 'it is no longer a matter of saying: to create is to think – but rather, to think is to create and primarily to create the act of thinking within thought. To think, then, is to provide food for thought.'[6]

To return to our title, it is this *thinking*, and its acts, pronouncements and changes-to-mind, that can create political and tactical responses and actualities. Indeed, at school we might have been called a 'keener' or 'beaner' if we thought hard about a piece of work – or we might have called others this if they did – but these stigmas need not hang over into our lives as 'adult', 'independent', 'free' (whatever we like to think of ourselves as) thinkers. (And nor should the 'results' we got at school, so often representative of amenability to structures of testing, rather than the ideas we may have had, or tried to advance.) For the ability to think is an endowment of human existence and not a privilege granted singly to the 'intellectual' (so often so variegated a figure, of whom an aetiology becomes impossible to pin down or standardise when put under any scrutiny), policy-maker or public enunciator. It is through thought that we may become thinkers (which – as Deleuze has shown – is not a tautology), and we hope that these articles and writings within this book will serve as spurs to thought for our readers.

iii)

Harold Wilson famously said that a week is a long time in politics. This being the case, the time-lapse between the writing and original publication of the articles here presented and what's occurring *now* will no doubt be inescapably noticeable, but what should be perceivable as standing behind this is the indiminishable impetus and ethos of the politics here represented. That is, of a politics that is not 'floating'; on which, one brief word, in relation to media representations. Before the 2015 General Election a local news channel's 'gauge-o-metre' of public sentiment focused on a group of 'floating voters', congregating in a Bristol café and chatting policy, umming and ahhing – as if at a pageant – over who looked best; it was utterly unconvincing, seeming forced and dated (as if it belonged to the era of the TV debates, which has perhaps passed since 2010's election). What was lacking, however – and what made the article seem trite – was a distinction that could solidify the subject positions within the piece and make them seem a bit more realistic to the audience: the *scale* on which these voters 'float'. That is, is it between parties or political positions that they float? It was the latter that was unanimously implied. However, one's politics might necessitate a vote for the Greens – whilst they are left of a Blairist Labour Party, and have fixed political ideas in place, as opposed to the Lib Dems' displaying of a willingness to squirm any which way – but this could change, say, after Corbyn's leadership election, which alters New Labour into a new party, of the old Labour mould. In this example, one's politics can in fact be found to be stable, and it is the parties that vacillate. It would perhaps be a more interesting gauge to present an article in terms of a voter's politics and then put these in relation to the parties, and their Politics; it would at least put paid to the myth that sets up the Political spectacle itself as just another *X-Factor*-style competition.

What can be seen now is that in the political era to come – that of a kind of 'kinder' politics, which will remain for four years in opposition to the unkinder kind – genuine competition, with all the baggage that goes with that term, will return, through the shift back to defined party politics. It will be (and already is) how this is capitalised upon that we must look out for. What we are now seeing with Labour is the proof of opposition; something that has been lacking in the political hegemony of the past fifteen or so years. The rhetoric of the Tories will likely change, and is changing, due to this, from the blame-game being played against 'the previous Labour government' to the target becoming the current 'Labour opposition'. Cameron's employment of one of the lowest tactical smears of recent political memory – labelling Corbyn a 'security-threatening, terrorist-sympathising, Britainhating ideolog[ist]' – whilst being laughably parodic, is an early example of the showing of the serious threat felt by the governing party: it's no longer simply a bit of banter with 'Red Ed' at PMQs – whilst the tabloids do the dogwork of tearing him to pieces – the dominating party are now stooping to the level of the gutter press. This represents the real mania over Corbyn: the death throes of a media whose game is up. But it is perhaps only up in terms of the old tricks. What must be watched out for is the press getting savvy to this; it will likely become so that the smear of not singing the national anthem or bowing low enough at the Cenotaph will stop washing with the public and will be seen for what it is and maybe even met with the same dignity as Corbyn himself meets such with, but what this could be replaced with is scary: the imputation of any unrest or unruliness to the opposition party itself, which is supposedly so 'radical' ('radical-ising' will no doubt become the tune) and 'dangerous'. These imputations will be calculated and shameless, but what mustn't be forgotten is their *deflection*: if the pinch is felt, it must be noted that it's being administered by the party in charge, the inventors and implementers of current – and the long road ahead's – policies.

iv)

We have long been living in what Walter Benjamin called 'a culture of distraction'. However, politically, we now seem to be inhabiting something more like a *'politics* of distraction', which is crucially different. Whilst a 'culture of distraction' implies that culture distracts from politics (hype about the Super Bowl distracted from Bush's foreign policy, for example), by a *politics* of distraction we mean that we are now distracted from politics *by politics* (or, indeed, from Politics by politics). It is often when we feel we are most 'debating the issue' that we are least political, least critical and the most inside ideology.

In the case of Jeremy Corbyn vs. Martin Amis in UK 'official' and social media – the latter of whom said of the former that he is 'undereducated', 'humourless', displays 'slow-minded rigidity' and is 'essentially incurious about anything beyond his immediate sphere', to which the former responded that Tories are often 'over-educated and under-learned' – if we enter the debate, we already take a side: the side of a politics of distraction. It is too late, we are inside it now and so we must care about it (that is how this politics works). The Left is increasingly becoming aware that we should pay attention to the right-wing policies that are getting through parliament on the very day that we are in a fury about Cameron fucking a pig, but there is yet still more to this. A politics of distraction ensures that we waste our time becoming angry about things that will be gone tomorrow. Will we be talking about Amis in two weeks, or even two days? It is safe to say that we will not. A politics of distraction works to focus us in on a moment, on a temporary concern that gives us something to talk about over breakfast, but will ensure that we do not think politically in a long-term way.

Perhaps the question is why we cannot not leave these issues aside. Why is it difficult to realise that Martin Amis is an old sod whose comments aren't worth even pricking our ears up over, let alone treating them (very bizarrely) as a genuine threat to Jeremy Corbyn? (That is, Corbyn really and truly does not need the help of left-wing social media to overcome the critique of Martin Amis.) Or rather, how is it that we find it so hard to act upon what we know to be true here? We seem to realise this, but yet we continue to act, respond and discuss (largely on social media) as if we have not had this realisation, as if every story published by the *Guardian* must be responded to, and every comment from Martin Amis must be taken seriously.

Perhaps it is because the culture of distraction has trained us to be ready for this politics of distraction. Whilst we might praise the recent politicisation of social media, we must be wary of the social-media-isation of politics. This is what we must now fight against, a politics that denies us the ability to think carefully about what we care about and what we should discuss and instead forces us to respond furiously and quickly to a debate we see 'raging' on social media. Herein we might begin to resist. That said; in the spirit of Jorge Luis Borges, are we herein ourselves guilty of the very thing we criticise?

v)

Our politactical project, Everyday Analysis, aims to be neither 'hot-off-the-press' journalism nor long-term, long-form investigative academic or journalistic work. This, in itself, is nothing new, and in fact there is a growing trendiness in this area. One such example is the journal *The Conversation*, which has the tagline 'academic rigour, journalistic flair'. Yet, in some ways this tagline embodies the reverse approach to ours. *The Conversation* looks to bring together what is *best* in academia with what is *best* in journalism, seeming to have high regard for the traditional values of academic research and for the beauty of journalistic expression(ism). The result is that we end up with journalistic political and cultural articles, which also lay claim to legitimacy and expert status on account of the apparent 'academic rigour' behind them (the university of the author is listed below each article, lest we forget where these arguments are coming from).

Contra *The Conversation*, the aim of Everyday Analysis – with an author-anonymity that opposes it to such academic publications – is far from attempting to combine 'the best of both worlds' (the academic and the journalistic). In fact its aim is to counteract the dominant traditions in both academic and journalistic discourse. We attempt to encourage analysis *of* and work *against* the existing trends and the unconscious structures that determine academic and journalistic discourses and which hold both in high regard. Our articles do not come with academic authority, nor are they the first to *break* the news with a flourish. Some are written by academics and some by journalists; others by teachers, students and readers. Whoever the writer, these articles aim not to solve difficult cultural problems nor to offer the most conclusive assessment of them, but to break open assumptions about news stories and political events and their reception, pointing to unanswered questions in our reportage of events and in our often stranger-than-meets-the-eye responses to cultural and political phenomena, to the gaps and inconsistencies in our daily political lives and identities. This is a political tactics. In a way, we are looking for the *worst* of academia, the marginal and radical spaces in academic discourse not subsumed into its dominant traditions, but which put them into question. The cultural theorists discussed here are often those most troubling to the university and least popular within it. The idea of the university as an 'ivory tower' is an old one, but it is increasingly apparent that the world of journalism is no different. We want to bring these thorns in the side of academia together with what we can call the *worst* of journalism, a journalism that does not come with the cultural capital of big newspapers, but which troubles the traditions in media and can operate as a thorn in the side of the structures that govern how we read, consume and respond to the news. This operation of the thorn is what we have aimed at with *Politactics*.

Below, we tactically lay out our political articles and responses in order corresponding to our section headings: 'The Political Landscape of Britain: Materially and Symbolically'; 'Its Political Figures and Configurations'; 'In the Divided Kingdom'; 'States of Nations, and Nationalist States'; 'On Work and Leisure'; and an 'Afterword'. Responses to, or 'second opinions' on, the articles as 'case studies' – of varying number, length and intensity – are found below those which are being responded to, enumerated anonymously and randomly by a), b), c), etc.

2

The Political Landscape of Britain: Materially and Symbolically

Spikes, Shopping and Selfridges

Charles Baudelaire wrote of the 'religious intoxication of great cities', suggesting that the modern city appeals in an opiate way, as religion had.[7] Years later, Walter Benjamin wrote that Baudelaire was right, and that 'the department stores are the temples consecrated to this intoxication'.[8] For Benjamin the department store was a key part of the city because it taught or instructed the city's inhabitants how they should read the city as a whole: the department store seemed to embody something about the city's ideology. This link between the city and the department store has risen its head again in the past few days, with national newspapers reporting on the cruelty of Selfridges' 'anti-homeless spikes'.[9]

These metal spikes, which are termed 'defensive architecture', prevent homeless people from sleeping outside department stores. Selfridges claim that these spikes are a result of 'customer demand' not to be 'harassed' by homeless people whilst shopping. No doubt there is some truth in this: customers find it especially offensive to see a homeless individual in this particular place. But why should it be the department store that is the site for this problem? Why is it particularly offensive to see a homeless person on the way into or out of Selfridges, rather than anywhere else?

The department store is the perfect place to buy a commodity, and it sells no necessities. The stores are in fact a denial of the existence of necessity at all: they are worlds in which there is only indulgence, where everything is desirable but nothing is needed.

The stores completely separate *want* from *need*, and in fact deny the existence of *need* entirely. To be immediately confronted with someone in *need* outside Selfridges threatens the whole ideology of the store.

This celebration of the department store as a space of glamorous desire with no undesirable elements has made its way into popular culture in the last few years as well, with both ITV and BBC running major (ongoing) series about Victorian department stores, *Mr Selfridge* and *The Paradise* respectively. *Mr Selfridge* embodies this kitsch atmosphere (Milan Kundera defines 'kitsch' as 'the denial of all shit') with unsavoury aspects expelled and the untainted celebrated. The BBC title *The Paradise* avows the same thing: the department store is a place without undesirable aspects.

The spikes represent the failure of the department store to progress beyond Victorian attitudes to the poor (department stores saw themselves as breaking out of these class prejudices). In our age of austerity – a repeat of Victorian austerity – the poor are victimised and blamed (and Selfridges is back in our consciousness). It is another example of vilifying the needy.[10] Even the phrase 'defensive architecture' suggests that homelessness is an attack that needs combatting. Homelessness threatens the department-store ideology which depends on desire and excess, so evidence of the homeless outside Selfridges operates as a reminder of the falseness of this ideology and causes the consumer to feel guilty by reminding them of need and threatening to prevent them from believing in the magical and pure world of the department store (and the city).

a)

The popular outrage at installing spikes outside Selfridges has recently been matched by an equal and opposite reaction in favour of the decision by ex-Manchester United footballers Ryan

Giggs and Gary Neville not to evict a group of squatters from the building the pair recently bought in Manchester city centre. The Manchester Angels, a homeless support group, occupied the building in October 2015 and have been granted permission to remain until at least February 2016, when work will begin on transforming the building into 'a 35-bedroom boutique hotel complete with a gym, spa, roof terrace for members, and a ground floor restaurant'.[11] Giggs and Neville have reportedly provided showers, toilets and hot meals for those now living in the building.

If the spikes at Selfridges represent a persistence of Victorian attitudes towards the poor, then the decision of Giggs and Neville seems to represent an uncomfortable persistence of Victorian forms of charity. Why, many commentators asked, did it take two rich footballers to provide temporary housing for the homeless at a time when so many other buildings lie empty or underused?

This is a valid question, but it is worth approaching tangentially, by considering the history of the building in question: the Manchester Stock Exchange. This building originally opened in 1907 to provide a new base for the expanding trade activity of the existing city Stock Exchange. According to the building's Grade-2 listing entry, it is designed in an Edwardian Baroque style, with elaborate stone decoration and Art Nouveau railings.[12] Its origin, then, is as a bastion of capitalist circulation and accumulation; the kind of place that could be relied on to produce Selfridges customers. It has now been temporarily renamed 'the Sock Exchange', transforming it from a site of exchange-value to one of use-value. Socks are prosaic, unglamorous, necessary objects; in the language of the preceding article, they signify *need* rather than *want*. This redesignation can only be temporary, however, since from 2016 this building, which cost Giggs and Neville £1.5 million, will revert to the glamorous and fundamentally defensive architecture of wealth, becoming a boutique hotel complete with private members' terrace. It is while, and *only while*, the building is in an intermediary state that it can be countenanced as a home for the homeless. The occupiers have been permitted to remain, it is true, but they are existing in the interstices of capitalism, in the temporal gap between Stock Exchange and hotel. The decision not to evict can be equated to a decision not to erect spikes outside a department store. It is to be approved, certainly, but not to be confused with an act of genuine revolution. The really radical thing would be to allow the homeless to enter into Selfridges itself, or to stay in the new hotel once it opens.

In this case, the question raised above can be rephrased. We should not only ask why temporary housing is unavailable, but why and how land-use, defensive architecture and the deployment of capital renders temporary housing necessary in the first place. Perhaps most concerning about this series of events is that it shows we have reached a state where a mere negative act – a failure to evict, a failure to erect spikes – has come to appear as a positive act of acceptance.

Banter and its Vicissitudes

Suppose we take the recent rise and fall of Daniel O'Reilly, better known as Dapper Laughs, as an opportunity to examine the meaning of 'banter' in 21st-century Britain. It's an opportunity perhaps overlooked by us the last time the issue of 'banter' really became newsworthy, in the shape of former Cardiff City FC manager Malky Mackay's leaked text message exchanges with club sporting director Ian Moody. What are the threads that connect these two stories?

Firstly, they are linked by what we might call 'the banter defence'. Mackay's texts, which offered a wide spectrum of offensive content, bridging racism, sexism, homophobia and anti-Semitism, were explained away by an impotent League

Managers' Association as the result of Mackay's need to '[let] off steam to a friend during some friendly text message banter'.[13] During the ultimately successful online campaign to persuade ITV against commissioning a second series of O'Reilly's sketch show *Dapper Laughs: On the Pull*, those rallying around the cause opened themselves up to entirely unsurprising accusations that they lacked a sense of humour, that they were opposed to freedom of speech, that O'Reilly's threatening and exploitative misogynistic spiel was nothing more harmful than 'banter'. So the term 'banter' is an apotropaic issued to deflect criticism of the given individual's choice of language or conduct: so far, so self-evident.

The second aspect shared by these two events probably needs even less explaining: both centred around a white, heterosexual man who at the moment of crisis stood accused of wielding that identity against other, less privileged identities (I'd add middle-class and cis-gendered to the mix, but as far as I know there was no suggestion of classism in Mackay's texts and I don't fancy combing back through Dapper's Vine feed to locate examples of transphobia). One would not struggle to find opinions to the effect that those seeking to have Mackay and O'Reilly answer for their statements were simply failing to get in on the joke, and were imposing cultural politics on speech acts that wanted nothing to do with anything so serious. The obvious retort to this would be that language is never not participative in cultural struggle, particularly when it concerns power differentials between different fields of identity (like O'Reilly's jokes about groping and rape, subjects that address themselves to a frame in which the difference between men's and women's access to public space inevitably comes into focus), and even more so when that language is delivered from positions of privilege.

Banter isn't necessarily racist, sexist and homophobic. Banter as heartily social and non-serious speech (the *OED* uses the phrase 'good-humoured raillery') can exist independently of this prejudicial content. It's just that this isn't the most characteristic form that banter takes today. If we generously accept the notion that banter is a kind of free speech, in the sense of a speech whose parameters are wide open, whose direction is carefree and perambulatory, it should come as no surprise that banter tends to emit from and conform to the deep-seated prejudices of those who already have the loudest and most sustained voice in the cultural conversation. It is after all much easier for white men to claim space to speak merely for the sake of speaking; one thinks here of John Cage's line: 'I have nothing to say and I'm saying it'. Thus, though notionally a language of freedom, banter in practice quickly becomes a *policing* language, in the sense put forward by Jacques Rancière, and explored in Everyday Analysis' recent article about the politics of the Man Booker Prize.[14] In what is perhaps his best-known critical manoeuvre, Rancière distinguishes 'policing' from 'politics', defining these respectively as the force that *symbolically constitutes the social* and the antagonistic force that *disturbs this arrangement*.[15] Despite its supposed openness, banter tends to order its subjects in a way that rigidly enforces the social status quo. When banter is used as an apotropaic – it's difficult here not to think of the former Sky Sports football anchor Richard Keys wielding the term as an excuse for his accidentally broadcast attack on a female assistant referee in 2011 – its adherents thereby perform the characteristic policing gesture, as identified by Rancière, of ordering bystanders to 'move along! Nothing to see here!' Banter is both a vehicle and a code word for white male heterosexuals who wish to speak on matters outside their experience without fear of reprisal, which is to say, with authority.

Here we can turn to the contemporary literary theorist Sianne Ngai, in particular her 2005 book *Ugly Feelings*. Ngai rejects Fredric Jameson's much-repeated idea that late capitalism marks a period in which we see a 'waning of affect' across society as a whole – the famous thesis that all culture in postmodernism comes to us in scare quotes. Another aspect of Jameson's assertion, at least as interpreted by Ngai, is that it removes from the picture those affects that traditionally motivated workers' struggles against capitalism's more baleful effects: the 'classic sentiments of disenchantment' under the conditions of wage labour, namely fear, insecurity and anxiety. Drawing on Paolo Virno, Ngai emphasises by contrast that fear, insecurity and anxiety are now central to capital's project, manifesting as 'professional ideals' of flexibility, adaptability and casuality.[16] Affects that once comprised the experience of alienation from capital have not vanished in culture, but simply now serve capital's ends.

The banter complex, however, would like nothing more than for us all to buy whole-heartedly into Jameson's earlier concept (this regardless of the percentage of banter adherents that have actually read *Postmodernism, or the Cultural Logic of Late Capital*). Banter is a language that claims to be drained of any affect besides the mild one we might call 'banterousness', a mood in which conversation is experienced as unserious, uncommitted and open-ended. The curious thing in this respect is that banter is at its most 'banterous' when it seems motivated by truly pointed affective intensities, when it paints a picture of assumed racial, class or sexual superiority, and/or a fear of the other. A linguistic practice that insists on its own lack of sentimental or political substance, banter routinely seems to offer an outlet for extreme feelings of *ressentiment*, presumably fuelled by Ngai and Virno's 'insecurity, fear and anxiety', all feelings that once stood on the side of alienation but with which capitalism now makes itself at home. Banter today is commonly a language of antagonism which, through its spurious claim to a kind of wandering affectlessness, denies over and over that its choice of targets forcibly reproduces the way things currently are under capitalism. Which is to say, banter is first and foremost a language of emotional dislocation, a privileged language of alienation whose speakers characteristically misrecognise their own place in the scheme of social power. As such, banter takes its place in a much broader subcategory of discourses related to the fantastical 'oppressed majority', from Gamergate to UKIP.

Cover-Ups, Connectivity and Misrecognition

Misrecognition is not ignorance. Misrecognition represents a certain organisation of affirmations and negations, to which the subject is attached. [...] There must surely be, behind his misrecognition, a kind of knowledge of what there is to misrecognise.

— Jacques Lacan, *Seminar I*[17]

Smiley Culture's nephew, Merlin Emmanuel, reiterated the unofficial name for the British IPCC – 'the Independent Police Cover-Ups Commission' – at a meeting entitled 'Defend our young people, give them a future', which was held directly after the hottest moments of what were billed the 'UK riots', on 15 August 2011, at North London Community House in Tottenham.[18] 'Complaints' is of course the word that officially stands in the stead of 'Cover-Ups' in the organisation's name; however, when it comes to police forces the 'Western' world over, in specific relation to their – and their investigatory bodies' (often made up of former police themselves) – consistent failures to bring cops to justice over the killings of predominantly young, black, unarmed men, the replacement C-word is acutely resonant. As in Ferguson, Missouri, the trial for the killing of Michael Brown has returned the decision not to indict the police officer responsible for shooting him, Darren Wilson, and protests erupt all over the US, as well as in solidarity elsewhere, memories of the same result in the Mark Duggan inquest (skewed from the very beginning by the IPCC) are evoked.[19] And over the past few days another black child has been shot by a police officer in Cleveland, Ohio, for waving a BB-gun that the witness who notified the police albeit claimed was 'probably fake'.[20] Such stories abound, as they have over so many decades, and we're seeing responses to them being made – through uproar and protest – concerning structural institutionalisation of racism, and its slurry of cover-ups. Indeed, for there even to be conditions for protest chants, placard slogans and hashtags such as 'black lives matter' to necessitously come about demonstrates the need for not only the assessment but the upheaval and overturning of such conditions: as Martin Luther King Jr. famously said, 'injustice anywhere is a threat to justice everywhere'.

And now we are also beginning to see yet another slew of news items about seemingly State-sanctioned paedophilic crimes in the highest echelons of the British establishment. After the revelations concerning Jimmy Savile in 2012 and the spread of Operation Yew Tree's branches to hang so many celebrities out to dry, claims implicating more VIPs – including prominent Tory MPs in the 1980s – in *murderous* paedophilic crimes are coming out, and even being called 'only the tip of the iceberg' by Home Secretary, Teresa May.[21] As this media snowball rolls quickly into the avalanche it will become – picking up along the way the names of Dolphin Square and Elm Guest House, and the stuff of what yesterday could only be thought of as nightmare or conspiracy theory (the seeming impossibility of finding someone not linked in some way to the matter to investigate it, from the fiasco of Elizabeth Butler-Sloss to that of Fiona Woolf; the Dickens dossier pertaining to the ring, which conspicuously went missing from the Home Office; declinations by institutions such as the BBC to follow up leads they were alerted to by figures such as *Crimewatch*'s Jill Dando) – cover-ups of the past are shining a bright interrogatory light on the present.[22]

In the case of the abovementioned provision of evidence to the police concerning the Westminster paedophile ring, its whistleblower anonymously reported their information to the police only on the proviso that they were accompanied by journalists, from the *Mirror*, who would break the story. The reason for this seems to be the fact that there have of course been so many accounts of police ignoring or covering up such information, especially historically in these high-profile child sex scandals, and not least concerning the killing of eight-year-old Vishal Mehrotra in 1981, in connection with the ring.[23] Thus, the securing of the information's dissemination through the media is a necessary step, and in the age of high-speed information dissemination via the internet – whilst it has its own pitfalls (not least in terms of assurance of the credibility, validity and veracity of certain sites, though this is no more than an exacerbation of pitfalls of previous information ages) – the guarantee that news can immediately reach a wide public disturbs the old possibilities of its guarded management. There is no doubt then that the fast and vast disseminatory capabilities of internet connectivity have thus been able to sweep certain carpets – under which skeletons in cupboards have been swept – from under the feet of those in whose interests it has been to cover up home truths that hit home. Thus, the tightening of restrictions concerning the freedom of the internet by governmental and 'security' bodies in this respect is of course something that must be resisted.

However, there is also an issue in online dissemination involving something of what Jacques Lacan termed 'méconnaissance' – or *misrecognition* – that perhaps needs flagging and discussing. It puts paid somewhat to the theory of the six degrees of separation, in terms of social media.[24] Misrecognition being that involved in the mirror stage – in which the infant misrecognises themselves in their reflection, through the ego imposing a sense of autonomy and wholeness on that reflection – there is perhaps a similar misrecognition occurring in our social-networking worlds, which we are able to create and craft to such an extent 'in our own image' (with the almost unlimited powers of addition and deletion). There is then the risk of them leading us to believe that everybody else must be on the same (home)page as us. However, should – by whatever chance – we hit upon any number of online groups or communities structured around racism, classism or any form of oppression or exploitation, this should perhaps startle us into the realisation that it is the very structure, however unconscious, of the customisable individualisation of our online worlds that is able to keep such networks commonly hidden, or covered up, whilst they thrive in such close online proximity. Misrecognition, then – as an essential structuring element of subjectivity – should at least alert us to what's involved, and what can systematically be elided, in connectivity.

Policing Pornography/Policing Fantasy

On Monday 1 December 2014 new legislation was introduced which placed restrictions on what can be represented in Video-on-Demand pornography produced in the United Kingdom. The new rules bring Video-on-Demand regulation in line with the regulations for what can be shown in pornography sold in licenced sex shops. The legislation and its legal ramifications are discussed in some detail by the admirable obscenity lawyer Myles Jackman on his blog.[25] Essentially the legislation places restrictions on representing a seemingly arbitrary and disordered list of sexual acts, including face-sitting – anything but gentle head-scissoring – depictions of female ejaculation (and particularly its consumption), urination, anything but the most gentle sado-masochism, and fisting.

It hardly needs to be said that the regulation of pornography, as part of a wider set of discursive practices about sex, is a political act. Morality is always political. It determines what is visible and invisible in our representations of the world, what should be pushed out of sight as much as possible, what it is tolerable to think with impunity, and as a corollary of the latter, *how* it is possible to think with impunity. In this way the regulation of pornography is a police act, insofar as it determines the possibilities of our modes of discourse and thought, possibilities that we can still transgress, but often at our peril, at the mercy of the repressive state apparatuses.

The most obvious and most important political implication of the new regulations is their misogyny. Even a cursory glance at the list makes it absolutely clear that what these regulations penalise are both certain displays of women's pleasure and women's power in the sexual negotiation. The disparities are clear: gagging and deep-throat scenes with a man's penis in a woman's mouth are acceptable, but a woman sitting on a man's face is not. Sometimes the disparities are laughable: eating a man's cum, perfectly acceptable, but eating a woman's, no, that is, apparently, perverse and depraved (these are the actual words of the Obscene Publications Act). I want, in what follows, to discuss another political ramification of these new regulations of pornography. On the issue of women and these laws I would rather highlight some women's voices who speak with more knowledge and authority on the question of misogyny than I am able to. Women who make feminist porn have been interviewed about this by *Vice*; the pornographer Pandora Blake has discussed the politics of the ban at length on her 'NSFW' blog; and the erotic film-maker Erika Lust has added her voice in the *Independent*.[26]

I can do no more here than further draw attention to their work. Rather, I wish to discuss another political facet of these new regulations: their policing of fantasy more generally.

It is, as ever, important to bear in mind the fact that the regulation of pornography is not a *simply* repressive act, though it is a repressive act nonetheless. It is not enough to simply say we are returning to 'Victorian morality', whatever that means, or to suggest that this ban is in some way isolated from other political concerns, that sexuality is not intrinsically political, and that its repression does not *produce* other forms of political subjectivity. It is not a closing of representations, but a redistribution of them in the interests of power. As Michel Foucault puts it in *The Will to Knowledge*, the question is to 'define the regime of power-knowledge-pleasure that sustains the discourse on human sexuality in our part of the world'.[27] These regimes are multifaceted and demand to be analysed in some detail rather than uncritically saying, 'this is a backwards step, sex should be open and now it's not'. Handwringing about repression is not enough; the object of analysis is to ask what this repression does politically, for repression in itself is not intrinsically negative. Indeed, in order to experience sexual pleasure, repression is absolutely necessary. As Roland Barthes states, 'a little prohibition, a good deal of play' (and Georges Bataille too always stresses the essentiality of taboo in sexuality).[28] One obvious production of these new repressions is the demand that the relationships between men and women as subjects are produced in a certain way. The message is not that pornography is banned, but that it must be produced in certain ways, which in turn produce the subject and the body in certain ways. Inseparable from the prohibition of certain acts is the prohibition of various manifestations of women's power in sex, which can in turn be linked to the Tory government's opposition to gains in power for women in society more generally (there is always implicit in the regulations something of a critique of masculine masochism, which perhaps has been seen as male weakness).

I want to discuss another form of political subjectivity that these regulations impinge on, a political subject who is closely related to the feminist subject: the fantasising subject, who can be a man, a woman or somebody who does not subscribe to that binary. I wish to adopt this particular emphasis not to suggest that the feminist angle is in some way less important – indeed, my own analysis is entirely predicated on the primacy of the feminist angle – but rather to stress the ways in which the regulation of sexuality by power moves subtly towards regulating subjectivities and experiences in the most multi-faceted and unexpected of places.

There is a sort of vague though unconvincing justification for some of these restrictions, based on an erroneous notion of public safety. As the *Independent*'s coverage of the restrictions points out, some of the practices that are banned are so because they are 'potentially life-endangering', though it is very difficult to see how face-sitting, female ejaculation, or any sort of responsible sado-masochism is likely to endanger people's lives.[29] On the other hand, the regulations seem to actually be in place in order to 'protect children', despite the fact that, as Myles Jackman reports, extensive research across the EU found no evidence that sexually explicit material does harm minors.

In the conjunction of pornography, its regulations and its viewers then, what is being constructed is a viewing subject who needs to be kept safe, not from pornography itself, not from seeing sex, but from some sort of unclear harm that certain acts supposedly pose which are somewhat divorced from the concept of pornography itself. This logic cannot maintain even a resemblance to a coherent set of safety principles, and where they cannot be maintained, they can be shielded from critique with the politically unquestionable logic of child protection. No politician, very few public voices in general, would dare be accused of supporting something that damages children, even if there is strong evidence to suggest that the thing in question is actually quite harmless. Though, indeed, the whole question of child protection seems frankly so absurd as to be discounted anyway. We are dealing with material that it is going to be difficult for any child to come into contact with. The pornography that has just been regulated is paid for, and thus requires access to a credit card, and besides, far more violent material is shown every day in the far more easily accessible medium of

Hollywood cinema.

The safety argument also seems to misunderstand the use of pornography. For most of its consumers, porn isn't some sort of how-to guide, very few people go to the effort of recreating complex sado-masochistic scenarios in their dining room with a multitude of equipment (of course some people do, but this is another form of political sexual expression whose terms are outside the scope of this piece). Rather, pornography is a tool of fantasy.

Often pornography works only to create fantasies that reinforce inequalities and violence in our society, though I wonder, unsure, whether there are not ways of experiencing even that pornography in subversive and pleasurable ways, at least for some spectators. On the other hand, from the arguments and critiques of the women who make feminist pornography, it can be inferred that a major problem with the current regulations is that they disproportionately restrict pornography that allows something else, whilst leaving intact that material that reinforces the unequal status quo. It is this radical porn that I am talking about in what follows.

Porn allows its spectators to fantasise sexualities outside their own terms of experience, to go far beyond what is available, or usually even desirable, to themselves in their everyday sexual negotiations and encounters. It offers an experience of sexuality that is not a form of compromise with the other, though that compromise has its own set of pleasures and intensities that the spectator of porn would never want to give up. Pornography is a set of visual practices and discourses that allow extreme, exciting, fantastical encounters with otherness.

These fantasies are not isolated either; they are not somehow cut off from the world. Pornography changes our interactions with our sexual partners, not in the form of a guidebook for how to have sex *like* porn, but in how we mutually think of each other, how we constitute each other as sexual subjects. And this is why it is telling that so many women who make feminist pornography have spoken out about this, because these regulations are attempting to restrict a resource for fantasising about different power relations in the sexual experience, and thus to restrict fantasy's ability to impinge on altering those power relations.

This in itself is political. Changing sexual power relations in our society is a revolutionary act. And if this constitution of safety, of the safe subject, by power, helps to restrict revolution in one key part of our social configuration, why should it not be part of a more general restriction of (non-sexual?) fantasy for other social configurations that intersect and interact with it? Fantasy is a constitutive part of all political change; to imagine other is a precondition of acting other, otherwise all that we have is what is currently given: a perpetual, homogeneous stagnation. It is telling that in the history of modern political repression, the safety of the political subject is so often conjured as a way of restricting revolutionary thought and change, from the Committee of Public Safety in the French Revolution to the Metropolitan Police repressing protests in the name of the safety of... who exactly? Not the people.

These regulations on pornography demand not the end of pornography, but rather that what is represented conforms more precisely to the power relations that already exist. It attempts to ban fantasising about other ways of living and relating. In the current political environment, pornography, as an easy target, vulnerable under the auspices of 'child protection', may only be the beginning to the policing of our fantasies.

a)

2014 marked a contradictory year for representations of kink in the United Kingdom. Legislation restricted the distribution of kinky pornography mere months after the *Fifty Shades of Grey* trailer became the most-watched film preview of the year. We, as desiring subjects, are evidently faced with numerous contra-dictory interpellations. On the one hand, the heteronormative interpellation seeks to deny the value of certain types of kinky pornography. It asks us to reject 'perverse' sexual practises in favour of monogamous partnerships and nuclear families. On the other hand, the neoliberal interpellation sustaining the Hollywood blockbuster model of corporatised, global cinema urges us to value representations of the very 'perversions' deemed transgressive. As the writer of 'Policing Pornography/ Policing Fantasy' eloquently notes, 'handwringing about repression is not enough; the object of analysis is to ask what this repression does politically, for repression in itself is not intrinsi-cally negative'. In a similar vein, queer theorist Robin Bauer demonstrates how the polyphony of criss-crossing, contradictory repressions and interpellations produces excesses in processes of subjectification, and paradoxically 'opens up options for agency in the interfaces'.[30]

While female ejaculation and face-sitting are easy to identify as dangerous only insofar as any expression of female sexual pleasure threatens patriarchal narratives, it is essential to address the acts listed where there is a potential for real harm when practiced improperly. Our response to the difficulties of sexual investments in humiliation and violence, possibly an inevitable result of structures of discipline and control in contemporary society, must be to educate people on kinky practices and how they can be safely and responsibly enjoyed. Reading kink as inherently life-threatening or immoral collapses the ethical differences between consensual performances of power and non-consensual, traumatic abuses. This collapse of ethical difference has implications that extend into the sphere of all sexual relation-ships, leading to the bizarre situation where many claims of rape are dismissed as 'fictional', while consensual kinky performances are interpreted as 'real' threats to the social body. The overzealous policing of kinky fantasy and kinky sex is necessarily accompanied by a tragic inefficacy when it comes to the policing of instances of non-consensual, gender-based violence.

The writer of 'Policing Pornography/Policing Fantasy' comments that 'very few people go to the effort of recreating complex sado-masochistic scenarios in their dining room with a multitude of equipment'. Although many of them remain in the closet, there are of course large communities of people in the UK and beyond who own sex or fetish toys and who regularly engage in many of the acts censored by the 2014 legislation. Restricting the distribution of kinky pornography is not merely an anti-feminist regulation of representations of female pleasure, but a direct message to kinky people: *your ways of being intimate are wrong*. In response to this, we might ask: are the power dynamics of the heteronormative, vanilla relationship any 'safer' or more 'natural' than the dynamics of kinky fetishism or sado-masochism?

The *tableaux* of the nuclear family sat at the dining-room table is reproduced via the recreation of complex, sado-masochistically charged rituals. For centuries, women have been responsible for organising these rituals; producing food that will stimulate the senses without overwhelming them, setting the table so as to supplement the body with tools, and so on. Although few of us recreate *consensual, queer* sado-masochistic scenarios, many of us recreate *non-consensual, heteronormative* sado-masochistic scenarios in our dining rooms on a daily basis. (The women in my family are the ones who do the cooking and washing up, and the men are always given larger portions.)

It cannot be forgotten that many of the two women killed per week in England and Wales as a result of 'domestic violence' likely shared a dining room with the partners or former partners who murdered them. The dining room is not a 'safe space' that is threatened or invaded by consensual kink; rather, consensual kink provides us with ways of recognizing and re-ordering existing power relations. 'With its exaggerated style', concludes

Bauer, 'BDSM generally reveals that the social order is unnatural, scripted, and invented'.[31] Kink exposes the mechanics of the sado-masochistically charged, non-consensual power relations that are *always already* at play in our dining rooms, courthouses and political offices.

Furthermore, we might remind ourselves that even heteronormative sex requires a 'multitude of equipment', from chemical supplements such as Viagra, to prophylactics and birth-control pills. These cyborgian supplements cause us real pleasure and pain, and are no more 'natural' than a flogger or a nipple clamp. Following post-porn theorists such as Paul B. Preciado, we might question why the violence of an act such as erotic spanking is seen as more 'real' than the violence of high-heeled shoes, hair-removal treatments or cosmetic surgery. Indeed, why do we never speak of an unhealthy 'erect-penis fetish', a worrying 'cleavage fixation', or a dangerous 'heterosexual intercourse perversion'? *All* sexual acts have the capacity to be damaging, even the most seemingly vanilla ones; but in the same way that not all pornography featuring penetrative sex involves the violence of rape, not all pornography featuring erotic choking involves the violence of abuse.

Although kinky pornography might not always function as an accurate 'how-to' guide, I believe that it frequently provides us with a valuable form of transformative pleasure-knowledge. Kinksters have many lessons to teach us about how to navigate the difficult boundaries between erotic spontaneity and pre-agreed contractual obligations ensuring mutual safety. Current legislation focuses on a reductive binary of 'consent/non-consent' when it comes to sexual contact, and the DSM (*Diagnostic and Statistical Manual of Mental Disorders*) still defines many kinks as pathological. When our sexual consent is violated, many of us know we cannot go to the police, because no medical or legal systems exist to account for the complexity of our social-political-economic interactions. Kinky communities have pioneered technologies of consent that respond to the fluctuating and often conflicting positions adopted by the desiring subject under late-capitalist patriarchy, developing nuanced rule systems such as Risk Aware Consensual Kink (RACK), Safe Sane & Consensual (SSC), Consensual Non-consent (CNC) or a 'traffic-light' system of safe-words. Kinksters often advocate lengthy preliminary negotiations regarding 'hard limits' and 'soft limits'. These negotiations are often shown in kinky pornographic films, forming an integral part of the narrative of the encounter. In the words of one of Bauer's interview participants, the SM community

> is a community of […] folks who understand what it feels like to be non-consensually dominated or oppressed, queers and trannies and sex workers and people of color and working class, poor folks who understand that our gender's a creative response to our oppression. And our sexuality's a creative response and a healthy response.[32]

We are *all* caught up in complex sado-masochistic scenarios, whether we consent to them or not: gender is one such system, but there are many others. For example, Jeremy Corbyn's 'not-low-enough' bow at the 2015 Remembrance Sunday service made headlines in most major UK newspapers because the fetish objects and rituals of dominance and submission of a handful of (often white, cis-male) politicians were viewed as gestures of national or even global importance. Political, legal, military and religious systems rely on the same pornographic logic that imbues meaning upon certain gestures during spectacles of kinky play. By reading the Remembrance Sunday ritual as a 'scene' – in the sense used to describe a session of kinky sex – we simultaneously attest to the capability of bodily gestures to signify complex, political positions, *and* expose the strangeness of this particular 'scene' functioning as a newsworthy item. For, even by denying the political significance of a correct bow in front of the (inescapably phallic) Cenotaph, one inadvertently advances the political position of denying the value of national tradition. In response to religious rituals and military ceremonies, Corbyn was not permitted to simply say: 'YKINMK' ('Your Kink is Not My Kink').

As political agents, we are expected to respect certain rituals and revere certain fetish objects, but when we attempt to legislate alternate rituals or fetishes through kinky play or political activism, this is frequently considered to be insane or criminal. Certain types of bodily performance, such as those used at protests, are too often categorised into a 'legal/illegal' or 'violent/non-violent' binary that obscures the violence we are expected to submit to every day. In a similar fashion, while a woman can express non-consent to certain forms of sexual stimu-lation under current laws, she cannot easily express non-consent to other systems of oppression that might render her financially and emotionally vulnerable. Kinky pornography and the negoti-ations surrounding it render *explicit* (in all senses) the contra-dictory technologies of public and personal power relations, providing us with alternate figurations that are not only trans-gressive, but also potentially transformative.

3

Its Political Figures and Configurations

The Meaning of Michael Gove

To the Labour Party, Tony Blair is a difficulty. Its only leader to win two – let alone three – successive general elections is also the man who stained it with Iraq, the authoritarianism of his post-9/11 cabinets and the Mandelsonian intense relaxedness around the filthy rich. As anxious as the present party seems to be to distance itself from anyone identified too closely with New Labour, it is still haunted by the suggestion that it hobbled itself when it failed to choose the more Blairish of the Miliband brothers as leader. Blair's status is very different among the present Tories. On the cosmetic level, Cameron's supposed detoxification of the 'Nasty Party' was explicitly based on Blair's analogous muting of his party's traditional Left credentials, complete with the positioning of the ad-man 'heir to Blair' Cameron himself at its centre. At the level of policy, Matthew D'Ancona's account of life in the Coalition, *In it Together* (2013), describes a Tory inner circle captivated with Blair's memoir, *A Journey* (2010), which they read as a warning from a 'frustrated reformer' who came to regret not having forced more of his vision through during the 1997–2001 government when he had the mandate to back it up. A coalition of parties that got what seats they did on largely contrary election promises has a mandate for virtually nothing. And yet a desire to be more authentically 'Blair' than Blair has been behind the Tory-led government's commitment to forcing through massive and deliberately irreversible public-sector 'reform': a word which Perry Anderson notes has completely reversed its meaning in the past half-century.

In this party of two Blairs – the master of presentation and the would-be reformer – the Education Secretary Michael Gove has a particularly special position. It is a neat irony of the Tory attempt at detoxification that the party could only start to emulate anything like the common touch of the early Blair by appointing the most monochromatically privileged upper rung of the party in decades. By contrast, 'Oiky Gove' – as *Private Eye* imagines his colleagues call him – is a scholarship boy and the adopted son of an Aberdeen fish processor. Among the Etonian smoothies and city-boy spinners, Gove has the appearance of authenticity going for him: but this myth of Govean authenticity extends far further into his meaning for the Coalition.

Gove's mission for education reform has been consistently chaotic. Popular measures such as school-sport partnerships and Bookstart have been abolished in bouts of austerity-swaggering only to be partially restored after public outcry; plans for an 'English Baccalaureate' to replace the GCSE were leaked and also had to be shut down; flagship academies were being declared 'inadequate' by Ofsted well before the 'Trojan Horse' episode; disproportionate levels of funding have been found being thrown at Free Schools in a bid to shift them into the profit-making independent sector; and Gove himself has been the object of several no-confidence votes from teaching organisations, not to mention scandals over the bullying tactics and misspeaking of his aides. But ironically, in a Coalition where the appearance of conviction about anything beyond business interests is in short supply, even these embarrassments are rhetorically valuable. The key to Gove is that he appears to *really believe it*. This is the significance of the apparently eccentric hectoring and misapplied slogans from Cyril Connolly and F.R. Leavis, and the identification with traditional syllabi and modes of assessment quite out of sorts with most research on effective learning.[33] As was the case with Andrew Lansley – who in his short stint as health secretary was permitted to run wild with a dystopian reimagining of the NHS, only to be demoted when it became a PR liability – the current Tory Party actually needs these figures of dead-eyed commitment to dampen the perception that they are all just charmers and spinners who only care about protecting the interests of their rich friends. The Goves and the Lansleys retain this value even when they fail, because one arm of the Tory interpretation of Blair always has to be qualified by the other.

Gove's reforms are a curious combination of the economically latitudinarian and the intellectually prescriptive, revelling in a deregulated heteroglossia of competing education providers while demanding ever-greater stricture over what actually gets taught. What the myth of Gove's authenticity covers over in this is the unanswered question of why the dogma of consumer 'choice' should apply to education at all. Parental lobbying over how schools are run is a welcome part of democracy, but the finer points of pedagogical technique are scarcely something most parents would claim much working expertise in. Why indeed should they, when one of the benefits of a public sector is that it means we don't all have to be discerning shoppers when it comes to traffic-light systems and flu jabs, but – ideally – can appoint congenial people who do know about them to manage them for us? Education is just a peculiarly emotive example of such natural monopolies that affect us all, and which do not benefit from the marketplace's adored 'choice'. The 'Trojan Horse' episode says far less about a decline of homogeneous British values – as the authentic Gove authentically claimed – than it does about the consequences of imagining that education provision can be safely left to the marketplace, where anyone with the cash can stake their claim.

a)

Gove's authenticity in some ways follows the 'existentialist' logic that the philosophy professor Abe Lucas (Joaquin Phoenix) adheres to in Woody Allen's *Irrational Man* (2015), in which the authentic act is set up against the anxiety-ridden 'freedom' of choice (choice, that is, between so many different ways of doing nothing). Once resolved on, the act alleviates all anxiety for the character; so unmediated is his belief that it escapes beyond all dialectical rationalisation, beyond the categorical imperative, beyond the realm of the Good, into the teleological suspension of the ethical: the murder he commits he's so committed to, disenabling him to see outside of its project to its consequences. Under Gove's reign, many educators may similarly have felt that they – and the consequences of his reforms – were not seen outside of the inner circle of his determined project.

b)

On 15 July 2014 Michael Gove was replaced by Nicky Morgan as Education Secretary. This marked the end of four turbulent years in charge, during which he oversaw changes that will have huge knock-on effects for many years to come.

During his time in charge Gove was responsible for overseeing the government's 'Academies' programme swell from encompassing around 200 academy schools when the Con-Dem coalition came to power in May 2010 to more than 4,500 by September 2014.[34] 'Free Schools', another Conservative innovation, saw around 300 new schools open between September 2011 and 2015, with another 100 slated for opening in 2016.[35] These are schools that can be opened by any provider, regardless of educational background. Requests for Free Schools to be opened by organisations such as Christian Scientists and Scientologists have, thankfully, been turned down, but there is an alarming array of groups now running schools that do not need to be staffed by qualified teachers or teach the National Curriculum.

The requirement to ensure that staff in school are qualified was abolished early on in Gove's reign. In a press release from 2012 the Department for Education stated that: 'Free Schools can hire brilliant people who have not got qualified teacher status (QTS). We are extending this flexibility to all academies so more schools can hire linguists, computer scientists, engineers and other specialists who have not worked in school before'.[36]

Indeed, it is this kind of thinking that seemed central to Gove's view and contributes perhaps to the negative views about him held by most practicing teachers. Gove frequently went on record to promote 'rigour' in schools. He wanted children to learn facts and called for a greater emphasis on rote learning, placing little value on current practice that placed importance on teaching children to *understand* the skills they were learning.

It is undeniable that wanting schools to be 'rigorous' is a worthy aim, but the method by which Gove set about achieving this underlines his lack of understanding of education, and more fundamentally the processes of how children learn. Bringing in experts in a field is all very well, but unless those people, gifted as they may well be, can impart those skills to young children effectively they have no purpose in a school classroom.

A product of this drive for greater rigour was the new National Curriculum, which became compulsory in schools across the country in September 2014. This document outlined standards for each year of the primary school and changed, radically, the methods teachers previously used to assess skills. Children were now to be assessed against a series of expectations for each year group, the standard of which was far higher than anything previously. Gove had zealously proclaimed that the new framework would stamp out 'coasting' schools and ensure that all schools were forced to reach his new benchmark of 85% of children achieving the expected level.

This again seems like a good idea in principle, but there are factors that make this extremely difficult. Firstly, he takes no account of the needs of schools who have intakes experiencing high levels of social and economic depravation. An 85% target is enormous when you consider that some of these children begin school speaking other languages, with minimal socialisation and often have parents who are unable to fully support their learning themselves.

Another important fact is that despite Gove's proclamations of a high-standard National Curriculum, the document published in 2014 is not actually compulsory in Academies and Free Schools, which now comprise a significant number of schools in England. These schools have total freedom to put together their own curriculum, assessed in whatever manner they deem appropriate. Despite the illusion of a National Curriculum, what actually exists is a curriculum for maintained schools, the type the current government would rather be rid of altogether.

c)

Gove's authentic belief in reforming education, as described through the lead article and responses, has coincided with the acceleration of a drive towards 'excellence' in all forms of education. Even though Gove is no longer Education Secretary, this approach lives on. Excellence, in its current manifestation, does not just mean being good at something; it means *being better at something than others in ways that can be measurably compared.* That is, it both requires and supplies the justification for an acceleration of competition. This outlook is encapsulated in Ofsted's reclassification in 2012 of its 'satisfactory' grade for schools as 'requires improvement'. This, the organisation states, is because 'only a good standard of provision can ever be good enough'.[37] It is only one step further to say that only excellence can ever be good enough. In such a system, which replicates the wider logic of capitalism, success is always predicated on the failure of others. Failure becomes the raw material out of which excellence is built. Excellence is particularly suitable for achieving this goal because of its malleable vagueness. It seems uncontestably, objectively, to be a good thing, whilst simultaneously remaining remarkably open to reinterpretation by those in power.

Higher Education has now become the focus of this Govist crusade for excellence. The existing Research Excellence Framework, which assesses research produced by staff in UK universities and awards funding accordingly, is due to be joined by a Teaching Excellence Framework (TEF), as proposed in a Government Green Paper in November 2015. This proposal has been put forward by Jo Johnson, Minister of State for Universities and Science, and the brother of Boris Johnson. Boris, we might observe, is the Conservative politician who is furthest from Michael Gove's attitude of ardent belief – his danger is that he gives off an aura of never really being committed to anything, of always speaking off the cuff. According to the Green Paper, the TEF aims to 'recognise and reward high quality teaching'.[38] But it is the way 'high quality teaching' is measured, and therefore how 'low quality teaching' is defined, that is the key issue here.

This becomes clearer if we recognise that 'excellence' has become a central part of what Adorno called the 'jargon of authenticity': the production of a vocabulary that seems to signify authentic truth, but which 'goes hand in hand with a vagueness that puts [it] at the disposal of any number of meanings in the disenchanted world'.[39] The value of excellence is that it combines apparent authenticity and conceptual vagueness, in the same way as the modern Tory Party can (and perhaps must) combine Michael's Gove's authenticity and Boris Johnson's vagueness. Teaching excellence therefore takes on a ring of incontrovertible truth whilst remaining a form of jargon open to manipulation. This combination also serves as a definition of ideology.

On the 'Freudian' Cameron

So, does David Cameron really 'resent' the poor, as per his allegedly 'Freudian' slip during his address to the Conservative Party Conference on Wednesday 3 October 2014?[40] Did his tongue lap into his unconscious and return with what he really thinks, which 'we' all 'knew' in the first place? Is this, at last, confirmation that the Bullingdon Club really is the id of the Party, the door barely closed against this storehouse of vicious and punitive elitism?

If one thing is more predictable than Tory gaffes in 2014, it's liberal glee at Tory gaffes. You can ascertain this in, say, the minimality of the interval between Boris Johnson fucking up in public and Another Angry Voice turning the fuck-up into meme which, if you were to believe the vast number of people who share it, penetrates to the core of a klepto-aristo-plutocratic *coup de main*. In every error, 'we' take pleasure in the crass ineptitude and, for that matter, crassness-in-itself, of 'them', taking it as an undeniable sign that 'they' have been forced right onto the electoral ropes.

But, as an individual, or even as a representative of a group of individuals, David Cameron almost certainly does *not* lie awake at night resenting the poor. He doesn't personally blame the poor for his lot; in fact, one would probably be fair in assuming that he can happily, if rather dreamily, envisage a Tory-utopian scenario in which *nobody* is poor because *everybody* is, by his definition, 'hard-working'. His aetiology of poverty might be ludicrously underthought, but that should not be confused with any common definition of 'resentment'. What it would be fair to say is that ideology – specifically neoliberal ideology – has to produce hierarchies of deservingness in order to legitimate its own uncon-cealable inequalities. If it 'resents' the poor, it does so in an entirely stylised way, a performance – even if that role is method-acted – of loathing which stretches across the Real that is neoliberalism's structurally essential material imbalance. It would be easier to think that Cameron's government hates the poor, in other words, than to come to terms with the fact that poverty is a necessary condition of our socio-economic life-world.

Maybe, then, Cameron's error needs to be read as a Lacanian, rather than a Freudian, slip. It was, of course, at another conference, in Rome in 1953, that Lacan made the memorable declaration that the Freudian cadre was, perhaps insurmountably, not Freudian enough. I've long believed that *'les non-dupes errent'* was the smartest of Lacanian formulae insofar as it militates for a rejection of the 'false-meaning/real-meaning' binary that has besmirched Freud's legacy in popular culture. Modern British liberalism provides an endlessly extending vista of *non-dupes* revelling in their self-anointed interpretative brilliance, as though it were enough on an analytical level to simply point out that Britain is becoming increasingly unequal and its Welfare State is being dismantled. 'We' can identify with the jejune obviousness of Banksy or Cassetteboy's ultra-limited satirical visions, or we can disarm the spectacular power, the curiously immobilising force, of Tory errors by critically addressing the way they speak to our own desires and resentments.

a)

The above contribution seems so much the more important in light of further 'slip-ups' on Cameron's part, related to his 'Bullingdon Club' past. The recent Great Big Pig Saga, or '#piggate' – a controversy in which it emerged that Mr Cameron may have put his penis into the mouth of a dead pig as part of an initiation into one of his elite clubs – has again raised these vital issues surrounding the often inadequate response of the Left to the lunacy of the elitist Right.

The article above hits on a point worth sustaining at the

second paragraph when it points out that (a) there is nothing shocking about these 'gaffes' and in fact we expect them from our caricatural right-wing figures, and (b) the left-wing glee on social media when such gaffes occur is probably the one thing that is even more predictable.

One particularly Freudian element of this situation is the humour of it. Speaking of George Bush, Lacanian theorist of comedy Alenka Zupančič makes a point that we ought to apply to some of our own chuckles at the likes of Boris Johnson and David Cameron's foolishness. She writes:

> Bush humour, with which he likes to demonstrate his ability to laugh at these miracles of wit that he keeps producing, is already a refashioning of the self-undermining power of 'Bushisms' themselves into a conservative way of accepting and tolerating pure stupidity.[41]

As was the case with George Bush in the US, in the UK today we are always waiting for the next gaffe on the part of our right-wing ruling elite. Bush harnessed this humour and used it to further entrench his power, just as Boris Johnson does, establishing the idea that whilst he is a fool, he is also a man of wit and intelligence who has the ability to laugh at his own mistakes and who even (more dangerously) shares a sense of humour with the purportedly left-wing glee that revels in his failures. The Left needs to be careful in its gleeful response to these cock-ups because they can easily be sucked into the trap of simply joining in with this 'conservative way of accepting and tolerating pure stupidity' that Zupančič describes. Cameron's gaffes, far from being shocking, are expectantly met with delighted and revelling internet memes rather than political outrage or opposition. This is a vital point about Cameron's Freudian slip, but it might not quite cover what needs to be said about the Pig Saga.

This 'gaffe' is a bit more giant, and its humour may go further than this liberal glee. Indeed, Cameron will not be joining in on the joke as Bush and Johnson so often do with their own collections of (sometimes arguably only slightly) more minor *faux pas*.

The media was quick to point out that there is something strangely prophetic about the Pig Saga given that the first episode in Charlie Brooker's famed 2011 *Black Mirror* series explored the idea of the Prime Minister being forced to have intercourse with a pig by terrorists who insisted on the act as a kind of ransom for a kidnapped national princess. There, the act of intercourse with the pig was symbolic of the ultimate defamation, after which one could no more sustain one's identity as a powerful and patriarchal masculine Prime Minister (the final scene of that episode showed the subsequent failed marital sex life of the PM). Here, on the contrary, sex with a pig is part of inauguration into this very club (the other people present when the pig was purportedly penetrated are also in powerful political positions). It at least suggests that these 'shaming' acts of self-defamation, such as one might find at the (slightly less so but still obviously elitist) initiation ceremonies of university Rugby Union teams, are not so much about the defamation of patriarchal power but about the establishment of it.

The incident reminds us that politics works by a patriarchy not dependent on having personal power, but upon the construction of a closed group. The initiation ceremony gives each member something over the others (something that would spoil their political career if it was revealed). This doesn't so much weaken their political power (by threatening to come out) but establishes it (by binding a group to each other).[42]

This event will stimulate the (probably already occurring) phasing out of Cameron. As Mark Fisher has been suggesting, this may serve the conservative agenda fairly well even if it isn't part of the plan. What we are not supposed to see is how the initiation ceremony initiates a power structure. Perhaps even further, it links capitalism to patriarchy as two wider structures produced by similar exchange-based acts which allow members to hold each other to ransom. Whilst for Charlie Brooker the imagined threat may have been an outside radical body forcing the inside of the political sphere to defame itself and lose its power, here the most horrible thing about our political structure is the ransoming within it which establishes its power.

The Election 2015 and the Manufacture of Media 'Objectivity'

Everyday Analysis has been a little 'Lacanian' on current issues recently – not least the General Election – remaining silent whilst the chatter continues all around and seeks to solicit responses, not to mention votes. With all the *X-Factor*-style playing-to-the-gallery in the media so far, the election-campaign machines this year have more than of late cottoned on to the atmosphere of voterly vacillation and sought to plug the electorate's desiring-machines back into the social-, 'political'-, *choice-*, big Other-machine of full-on canvas saturation (to use a little Deleuze/Guattarian terminology). But what of this voterly 'vacillation' itself?

To take one of so many ways in, we might discuss Ed Miliband's agreeing to an interview with Russell Brand for *The Trews*, lambasted on the front pages of the established newspapers before the interview was even broadcast, from being described as a 'gamble' by the *Guardian* to the right-wing rags toeing David Cameron's line of branding Brand a 'joke' – whom he 'doesn't have to hang out with' –, Katie Hopkins *et al* of course forming his celebrity coterie, as the *New Statesman* states.[43] But the *New Statesman* here somewhat misses the mark too, for what is implicit in most of the reportage is the dismissal of Brand – recently voted the world's fourth most influential thinker in a *Prospect* poll – as a 'celebrity', whereas in his capacity as producer of YouTube content and feature-length documentary the vacuity of *fame alone* being his sole defining characteristic hardly stands up, regardless of whether it may ever have.[44] To say nothing of the episode of *The Trews'* content (the idiocy of the prior speculation around endorsement and conversion speaks for itself), which was to be expected (Brand does not renege on his position; Miliband argues his points; there will be other interviews with leaders – of the Greens, for example – dependant on who accepts the invitation), the Labour spokesperson who stated nothing more than that Miliband 'had done an interview on Monday night' brings us closest here to an analytical vantage-point.[45]

The treatment of *The Trews* in this statement, as a media outlet, and of Brand as a journalistic interlocutor, is alien enough to the rest of the hyperbolic reaction from the mainstream TV and print news organisations (who see themselves, or rather endlessly strive to present themselves, as journalistic interlocutory media outlets) to show up clearly the very mechanisms at work here: the hegemonic attempt at expulsion of *The Trews* (and anything like it) from recognition as media or journalism. An expulsion, that is, from a carefully crafted *'objectivity'* the definition of which mainstream media has itself imposed, in an attempt to delimit parameters of public perception.

When Mark Fisher talks of 'the picture the reality managers have fed us for the last few years – the three "big" parties each offering a slightly different version of capitalist realism', he thus highlights very precisely what has been at stake not only in the manufacturing of a political assertion that has been slid into the place of 'objectivity' (i.e. 'capitalism *is* realism') post-Crash, but also the occurrence of this in media representation surrounding this election, and of course in reportage generally.[46] To bring what has been perceived as voterly vacillation (based on the occurrence of coalition and its likelihood again) back in here, it is maybe because of the rise of 'alternative' media, like Brand's *The Trews* and so many other online resources now, that the voting populace is becoming politicised, or politics-literate (political literacy being something disenfranchising governments and elites have been happy to see low, *amongst certain populaces*, when seats were safe). Indeed, this begs the question as to why our education and established media institutions haven't instilled this kind of political engagement themselves previously in the public, and of what might have been behind this disenfranchisement...

At a recent hustings event a candidate for the Greens emphatically encouraged voting for 'what you believe in'; it is paradoxical that the voting system of Proportional Representation, which the Greens are committed to (and which the treacherous Liberal Democrats promised to have a referendum on, but then simply shrugged off when in 'power') would be needed to be in place *a priori* for this to be really possible. Thus the recognition, and then dismantling, of *tactical-voting realism* and hegemonic media-manufactured 'objectivity' – through a rise in alternativism – might be our best hope for ushering in a challenge to the state of affairs that Brand has described as the 'rigged game'.

a)

One of Lacan's little formulations is that 'there is no metalanguage'. It is how he explains another, more complicated, one: 'that there is no Other of the Other'.[47] If we take an instance from a recent political event and its media representation we might be able to unravel some of the complexity here. In a powerful speech denouncing the ruinous economic policies of the Chancellor of the Exchequer George Osborne, John McDonnell quoted from Mao Zedong's 'Little Red Book' and threw over a copy to Osborne.[48] It may have been an apt quote, in relation to the Autumn Statement's fantastical figures ('we must not pretend to know what we do not know'); it may have drawn attention to the government's current relations with China; and it may have provoked a larger peripheral focus on the economic debate and Osborne's U-turns than would have otherwise occurred, through magicianly misdirection; but it was also unsurprisingly criticised heavily in the media.

More interestingly, in a metanarrative mode, some of the comment centred on 'the spin opportunities' made available by the 'stunt'.[49] One such instance was in a conversation on LBC Radio between Iain Dale and former spin doctor and Gordon Brown advisor, Damian McBride, who stated: 'frankly, not to sound like Chairman Mao, but I'd take that person [who gave the brandishing of the book the go-ahead] outside and shoot them!'[50] References to Malcolm Tucker from *The Thick of It* emerged too, and there was the air of the show's behind-the-scenes access to the event's surrounding talk, almost as if the discussion of spin was distracting from the spin itself. But what is elided in this type of talk are the positions it nonetheless refers to. It makes out there to be things there are not. In other words, talking of the event's spin opportunities implies there will be those who will spin the event and those who will be duped by this spin. It automatically hierarchically promotes the journalistic spin doctors to an overlordly position and relegates the potential audience to a plebeian position.

The question is, however, when this talk of spin is freely available to the public, who does the talk presume to be the public that this spin could hoodwink? Is it not setting up a straw public too idiotic not to be taken in by the spin despite a metalanguage commentating on it? In effect, this opposes the two Lacanian statements to each other. If taken rigorously, it can only be that either 'there is no metalanguage', in that speaking of spin becomes only part of it itself, or that 'there is no Other of the Other': if the Other is talking of this spin, must they not be making up an other Other – the gullible audience in thrall to it despite it being in plain view – that may not in fact exist? Perhaps it is rather that its discussion in plain view can become one way of piercing the ideological façade...

Dark Polls: The Power of Compartmentalisation

We have highlighted the issue of the delimitation and compart-mentalisation of our online worlds and worldviews – and the uses to which these mechanisms can be put (quarantine as well as collectivisation) – previously, and we have, too, demonstrated that our autopoietic social realms nonetheless share impenetrable proximities with diametrically opposed spaces, often on the same web-based platforms, in the article 'Cover-ups, Connectivity and Misrecognition' (above).[51] Further, as Honour Bayes points out in her discussion of the shocked reaction to the 2015 UK General Election in *The Stage*, it's not only internet coteries that are affected, but social worlds in-the-world too.[52] Yet the immediate question arising out of this might not be so much how to reach beyond our echo chambers, but how to dismantle or reconfigure the very systems that allow them – systems conducive to *divide and rule*, whether they were intended to be so or not.

As far as social media is concerned, the problem is that Facebook and Twitter become instantly invisible to their users, as *systems* themselves. For example, person A might be 'on Facebook', as we say, as might person B, but there may be little chance of their ever connecting (unless they're related, or have requested connection due to the fact of having gone to the same school aeons ago. The old joke about being able to choose your friends but not your relations has often been extended to choosing your Twitter follows whilst not being able to choose Facebook 'friends', so often old relations with... differing views). Through the system's machinations person B thus becomes invisible to person A: their online worlds are created for them with targeted self-generating advertising based on their 'likes', nostalgic quotes from their favourite movies and lyrics from fave songs appearing – completely self-contained, with no hint of anything beyond them – constantly; worlds with no futures, just repeating pasts creating the present: the end of history.

Of course, the real world is like this too. Due to divisions based on whatever identificatory phenomena – from class to social enjoyments – although seen, persons A and B have become just as invisible, or unknowable, to each other. But systems in 'the real world' – as corrupt a system even as Rupert Murdoch's monopolised media – are nonetheless readily visible and available to both of our imagined persons, as they are to all who pass by newsstands (and can afford, or choose to flick through, a paper) or to those who turn on their TVs. Online, we can post the articles or petitions we find pertinent, we can start up our own thinkpiece machines, but we're so often preaching to the already converted. The risk of what Jean Baudrillard would call the 'hyper-reality' of our online worlds is that their compartmentalisations directly contribute to our own *mentalisations*: we see the world in a certain way – and we see *all* others seeing the world similarly – so that we're astonished when it presents itself so differently from our expectations, as it has done in the UK election. The opinion polls pooled from whatever compartmentalisations themselves predicted things so differently from the exit polls that the latter had to be met with hat-eating disbelief until the very last moments. Although Scotland's triumph and the deserved death of the quisling Liberal Democrats were quite foreseeable, the lumpen shy Toryism of the vote blindsided the opinion polls, but after the terrifying lurch to the right in the European election, and the maelstrom of mainstream-media scaremongering and lying to its public at full volume, not even the passion of the anti-Christ Nick Clegg's warnings a little late in the day about the threat of nationalism would have been enough to have saved us...

As exampled by the *Sun*'s front pages from a week before the vote, the coverage of this election was vastly different in its English and Scottish editions: they went with the headlines 'It's a

Tory' (with a picture of a swaddled baby Cameron) in England and 'Stur Wars: A New Hope' (with Nicola Sturgeon as Princess Leia) in Scotland.[53]

As happened in the final vote, if Labour were weakened overwhelmingly in Scotland to allow the SNP a landslide, the likelihood of the Tories getting in in England increased however-many-fold. The *Sun* upped its sway to get its own(er's) way. And all the wishy-washy 'hey, that's just the way democracy goes'-saying should now set itself the task of placing that very pronouncement on the political spectrum, given all such media spin-doctoring, and judge just how righteously guiltless it should remain feeling.

The thing about the 2008 credit crunch and its fortifying of capitalist realism is that it seeped into every recess and calcified there, even into unexpected ones. Since then – if not before – many of us have found new media outlooks, mostly online, that are not as brazenly right-wing as the mainstream televisual and print presses in the pockets of the government. (As this is being written there is anti-Tory protesting on the streets of the capital, not being mentioned in any light by the BBC.) With the advancement of technology for its dissemination too, a real alternative has risen up online and, online, challenged the media establishment. But the generation gap that has been left to open up and been left open to being exploited by the old established media may thus have been underestimated. With the closure of Woolworths, W H Smith may look like an anachronism on our high streets, but it is archaic spaces such as these that also need to be infiltrated with an alternative. It may seem a meagre plea, but what might new periodicals or newspapers of political and critical comment be able to achieve if available from such stores' shelves? Perhaps new media means could assist in getting them made: crowdfunding, and a petition for representation in newsagents, just like the Greens got for representation in the electoral debates...

For thought needs to be reclaimed by the people, from whom the attempt has been meticulously made to divest it. Beyond the government policy (hidden and announced) in which this is explicit, it might also be seen in clever 'banter' of panel-show comedians being prioritised over intellectual insight – on feedback loops like Sky channel's *Dave*, where satire becomes almost indiscernible through saturation (and note such politicised detractions as Russell Brand or Frankie Boyle, who then become grist to the mockery mill) – or the stagnation of an academia (which in its more arts- and humanities-based areas has of course been targeted by cuts) that closes its loop to those outside it: conferences' extortionate ticket prices invite neither public attendees nor unfunded registrations, and journal syndication is so extraordinarily restricted. Whilst there are the beginnings of free distribution alternatives, this is increasingly how the Idea looks in the time of its intellectual property...

With a little media liberation we might yet come to see the Idea more clearly and no longer have to stare into polls darkly.

Jeremy Corbyn and the Future of the Left

The odds at the bookies were not in Jeremy Corbyn's favour at the start of his Labour leadership campaign – for he came out of left-field – but for them to have remained so up until the last could only have been an oversight. The conditions and foundations were unarguably, unshakeably in place for his nomination and election in that he represents a desired – but as yet undelivered – new kind of politics, or even, rather, a perennial kind, which has not seen the light of day on the supposed Left for as long as its centre of gravity was displaced to its (oxymoronic) right wing.[54] People may often cite Tony Blair as the leader who put an end to Labour's wilderness years, but it was in fact under his premiership that the classic spirit of the party was lost. Socialistically, the putting of the party – in effect

– into the hands of its members is a radical democratisation the likes of which is rarely seen in British party politics; as Corbyn himself says of this planned enfranchisement: 'I don't think we can go on having policy made by the leader, shadow cabinet, or parliamentary Labour party. It's got to go much wider. Party members need to be more enfranchised.'[55] Across its early policy generally Corbyn's enfranchisements and redistributions have made eminent sense: thus, it will no longer be the people being (politically) disenfranchised, but the private owners of public services (e.g. under Corbyn's plan for renationalising the railways, once the franchises expire the lines will return into public ownership); and rather than the obligatory and often tokenistic 'reshuffle' in the shadow cabinet there has been a genuine redistribution and reappraisal of its function and its roles, exemplified in one instance in the creation of a ministership for Mental Health, a position filled by Luciana Berger.[56]

But by and large, and not unexpectedly, the press have not been kind to, nor even remotely decent towards, Corbyn. By and large:

> Fleet Street's political commentators are unanimous in urging the Labour Party to move back into the middle ground of British politics. [...] Its left-wing policies put off potential supporters [and they] have failed to come to terms with the profound social changes that have moved Britain to the right. Fewer blue-collar workers, increasing affluence and a consequent decline of working-class identification have all eroded Labour's popular base. [...] Unless Labour moves with the times, it will cease to be a national opposition party and be permanently confined to its declining industrial fastnesses in the north of England and Celtic fringe.[57]

This is not, however, a summation of the press's reaction today, but is that of James Curran's in 1984, in the introduction to the book of essays *The Future of the Left*. The themes prove not time- or era-specific, but perennial; that is, they are stock phrases and gestures to be wielded in response to a left-leaning Labour, or leftist party in general: media spin in which fear is created self-defensively through the media's own fear of having its own spinful powers rolled back. In some ways luckily, the majority of the press (mostly avowedly right-wing, but 'left' too, in the case of the *Guardian*) – exposed through their death-throe reactions to Corbyn as the band of trolls that they are – cannot but appear a parody of themselves. To take an example, and not of the *Sport on Sunday*-style trashing and thrashing that's invaded the tabloids, occasionally the broadsheets, and the front benches of the House of Commons too, but a slightly subtler one from Edith Hancock, writing in *City A.M.*'s 'The Capitalist', about Labour's anti-austerity economic policy:

Some of these brainwaves have become known as "Corbynomics", among which is a plan – coined The People's QE and taken from tax blogger Richard Murphy – for the Bank of England to print money and splash it on infra-structure projects.

Murphy explains: "If QE funding was used to fund essential infrastructure improvements across the UK... that could increase employment [and] create new business oppor-tunities".

Sound familiar? Maybe not.

But then The Capitalist doubts you're au fait with the British National Party's manifesto from back in 2010, which had a section on QE.

"We would have employed at least a significant element of the new funding to create capital projects and investment in new infrastructure... which would also have created real jobs."

Great minds, eh?[58]

It's one example among so many all-out desperate slurs and smears, but, like so many of them, it wears its dumbness on its sleeve. Is the argument of the piece insinuating that if an economic policy like 'The People's QE' comes in it will in effect mean the Labour Party has become like the BNP, that the BNP will in effect get into power if Labour does? Is it insinuating that Quantitative Easing's only prior mention was in the BNP manifesto? Is it insinuating Quantitative Easing is a racist, bigoted policy? Seemingly so. Note how the mention of 'The People's QE' transmutes into just a mention of QE in reference to the manifesto. The piece is seemingly suggesting there has only been one mention of QE before Labour's talk of 'The People's QE' and that was in the BNP manifesto; not, that is, generally in terms of public finance in the wake of the financial crash of 2007/8, not in the Japan of the early 2000s... In the 'Capitalist' article the decontextualisation of the BNP quotation, the contortion of facts, the confusion of argument, and the smugness of the unfounded comparison is laughable.

The future of the Left thus appears unlikely to be able to rely on much, if any, support from media outlets that should be on its side and is being openly attacked by the (majority of the) press which erects itself in direct opposition to it. Despite the ridiculousness of it, the ridicule will mount and mount, and it does have an impact, repetition being a dangerous weapon for entrenchment. However, it is the entrenchment of the press and the establishment that needs to be opposed in new and innovative ways and in direct and democratic ways and with momentum in grassroots and technologically advanced fields. This entrenchment has a name: neoliberalism. We mustn't forget that – as Owen Jones reminds us – 'when asked what her greatest achievement was, Margaret Thatcher answered without hesitation: 'Tony Blair and the New Labour. We forced our opponents to change their minds.'[59] The future of the Left relies on this entrenched neoliberalism's replacement, a new union, a

new communal and communicative imaginary, or united imagination and hope, to be put in its place; as Ernesto Laclau states:

The crisis of the Left, from this point of view, can be seen as a
result of the decline of the two horizons which had traditionally structured its discourse: communism and, in the
West, the welfare state. Since the beginning of the 1970s it is
the Right which has been hegemonic: neoliberalism and the
moral majority, for instance, have become the main surfaces
of inscription and representation. The Right's hegemonic
ability is evident in that fact that even social democratic
parties have tended to accept its premises as a new and
unchallengeable 'common sense'. The Left, for its part,
finding its own social imaginaries shattered and without any
expansive force, has tended to retreat into the defence of
merely specific causes. But there is no hegemony which can
be grounded in this purely defensive strategy. This should be
the main battlefield in the years to come. Let us state it
bluntly: there can be no renaissance of the Left without the
construction of a new social imaginary.[60]

a)

As some on the left correctly anticipated, Jeremy Corbyn's
victory has been taken by the media as an invitation to instigate
a sort of US-style culture war here in Britain.

Denounced as 'childish' by the ever level-headed *Daily Mail*,
and a 'disgrace' by Murdoch-owned, royal-phone-hacking media
cabal News UK (*The Times*, the *Sun*) for not singing – sorry,
'mouthing the words' (Jenni Russell, have a cigar) to – the
national anthem, Corbyn's largely centre-left policy platform has
on the whole been ignored.[61] The press instead have opted to
play the man over the ball.

How has it come to pass that the limits of acceptable debate in this country have become so narrow-waisted as to make a Victorian socialite gasp? Why is there not a credible, established mechanism by which a republican can serve as the leader of the opposition without being subject to this sort of blanket character assassination by the press?

As it turns out, it's our own ruling class who are merely mouthing along to the tune of tolerance, while organising to vilify anyone who dares swim against the political tide. As the Tories' deplorable um-ing and ah-ing over the Syrian refugee crisis has shown, acceptance of cultural and indeed intellectual diversity is only a part of the cultural mélange of modern Britain so long as it knows its boundaries, both literal and metaphorical.

So what can team Corbyn learn from America, where this sort of divisive politics has a longer history? The reach of the Murdoch empire stretches far across the Atlantic, where the American culture wars play out more traditionally over his own cable TV network Fox News and its nominally left-wing counterpart MSNBC, rather than in print.

When Barack Obama came to prominence during the 2007/8 Democratic primary season, the American Right mobilised immediately to undermine his campaign, whipping up controversy over such banalities as his middle name (Hussein), his citizenship and even accusations over his apparent refusal to say the Pledge of Allegiance, after a photograph that appeared in *Time* magazine – echoed in Corbyn's own anthem-gate at the Battle of Britain memorial service.[62]

Obama, having only been voted to the Senate four years prior, was still a relative newcomer to the national stage, and had until then been operating with the caution one might expect in the even more condensed political climate of Washington, perhaps with an eye to the future.

On the other hand, Corbyn never once considered he might one day be leader of the Labour Party, so ran his career as a grass-roots activist and his day job as a parliamentary politician in tandem, without ever resorting to anything as tactical or *politiciany* as doublespeak. In the fresh light of power, this might seem naïve, but his shoot-from-the-hip approach is what made Corbyn so attractive to the activists who gave him his victory. Without discipline, it might yet prove to be his undoing in the face of a media baying for blood.

Corbyn's dual role did occasionally appear to be untenable, as the party shifted away from its base to a more think tank-propelled model during thirteen years of office. But Corbyn remained faithful, with a view that, were the grassroots and Westminster ever to reconcile, the Labour Party would be the natural vehicle for that concord.

As Labour pulled right, it dragged the national conversation with it, and, during the Blair years, Corbyn and his allies on the left became increasingly marginalised within the media and the PLP. The party began to regard him the way one does a sort of eccentric but dear uncle – a little strange, but essentially harmless. When he secured his final nomination for the leadership contest a few minutes before the midnight deadline, the attitude within Labour was of giving the old dog one last bone; a token gesture to the old party from those now at the helm. Here we heard the early whispers of journalistic contempt – at this stage still fairly good-humoured, if a little condescending to an MP of over thirty-years' service.[63]

Once polls started to turn in his favour, however, so started the leftward triangulation expected from Andy Burnham, Yvette Cooper and Liz Kendall, with all three eager to convert what they could of the new membership into votes (though, by and large, their only tactic appeared to be the reintroduction of the word 'radical' into the Labour vocabulary).[64] When it became apparent that a Corbyn victory was all but declared, the gloves were off as the trailing pack – particularly the Cooper camp – went on the attack. The press too dropped the slapstick Red-Scare routine and began in earnest to pursue him with the kind of brute force previously reserved for paedophiles, welfare claimants and Ed Miliband.

Where Obama had practically a clean slate from which to launch his presidential campaign, the British media saw Corbyn's activist history as kindling with which to burn him into the national conscience as a Queen-hating, commie-pinko terrorist-sympathiser.[65]

Tactically speaking, the Right seem to have gleaned their approach almost entirely from the Fox News playbook, painting the Leader of the Opposition, and more broadly the Left, as a national-security threat, if not downright sympathetic to terrorist causes.

It's a matter of parliamentary fact that Corbyn rebelled against the party whip over 500 times as a backbencher, and with increasing frequency during the final term of the Blair/Brown era.[66] He voted instead with his conscience on matters of welfare and war, and spoke with his heart as a campaigner and critic of Western imperialism in the Middle East. But, having been condemned by the tabloid media for everything from a purported sandwich theft to his 'Chairman Mao-like bicycle', what most surprised many on the left was the *Guardian*'s reaction to the Corbyn surge.[67]

Unlike the *Mirror*, who were sympathetic but ultimately backed Burnham, or the *Independent*, who remained outwardly impartial but seemed to lean towards a Corbyn victory, the *Guardian* – Britain's most widely circulated paper of the Left – took a wholly different approach. The paper began its anti-Corbyn campaign long before anyone else even took him seriously, running with an often patronising, Blairite editorial line which pinned too far to the Right for comfort.[68]

It would be consoling to think that, in their ongoing effort to stay relevant in the unforgiving landscape of digital journalism, the *Guardian* backroom just wanted to get in early so they could say they disliked Corbyn before it was cool. But this was clearly a symptom of their uneasy role as a – sorry, *the* – voice of the broad Left, who considered it their moral duty to include all opinion from what they saw as the centre ground of left-wing thought. What stuck in the craw with many was their choice to effectively narrow the limits of how far left the debate was allowed to go, adopting a 'now now, children' approach in the face of Corbyn's increasing popularity and the obvious hunger for a more radical approach from a Labour candidate.[69]

Now, backed up by an incredible mandate and with a loyal support base willing to fight his corner, Corbyn has a genuine chance to remake Labour as a party of democratic socialism for the future. If the *Guardian* can't get behind him, at least in spirit if not on a policy-by-policy basis, then he has an uphill struggle in front of him.

There is still some small hope. The 2008 Obama campaign is, among many things, remembered for its innovative use of the internet and social media (particularly the burgeoning Twitter platform) as a tool to speak to its young activist base and help shape the campaign narrative. In the run-up to the election, Organizing for America (now Organizing for Action) set up Fight the Smears, a website dedicated to offsetting what it saw as unfair coverage of the Obama campaign in the mainstream media.[70] The site came embedded with a tool that allowed supporters to email their contact list, fact-checking each new rumour and gaining significant circulation.

Similarly, established groups such as Media Lens and newly founded ones like Corbyn: Media Watch and Media Vs Corbyn have a role to play in challenging mainstream narratives.[71] By being inclusive and balanced, and setting themselves up to respond with an almost task force-like speed and precision to each new slur, the young Left can put their considerable online know-how to use to grow these alliances and become an effective weapon in defending Corbyn against the ongoing media offensive.[72]

Online campaigning is now an established feature of our political landscape, and has been wisely employed by the Corbyn faithful to his favour thus far. It's going to be almost impossible to counter the reach of the right-wing media in this way alone, but with dedication and an eye on the lessons of history, Corbyn's premiership still has a glimmer of hope.

For all its innovation, the foundations on which the Obama campaign was built are old hat: the perception of honesty and down-to-earth charm, infectious sloganeering ('Jez We Can', anyone?) and the promise of real change. For Corbyn, it's going to be a matter of knowing when to stay true to your principles and when to concede for long-term gains, when to be civil and when to stick the boot in, of reading the public mood and gaining their trust, and importantly, of exposing the failed orthodoxies of the Right and showing the nation that another way is possible.

b)

Corbyn's prime-ministerial candidacy makes us think a little about where we sit as political 'radicals' of the blogosphere, left-wing papers and journals. Take, for example, a book working in a similar direction to ours, Mark Fisher's 2009 *Capitalist Realism*. The book took until 2013 to really start having a wide-ranging effect and it has become even more popular since then. Russell Brand's endorsement of the book in 2014 made a much wider public aware of it. Recently, the significance of the book seems to have been hammered home by social-media attention to the fact that the term 'capitalist realism' has been used by Jeremy Corbyn's shadow chancellor.[73] John McDonnell is now a major player in the Houses of Commons, and naturally we are hopeful that McDonnell and Corbyn might really change things. In the case of 'capitalist realism', is this a straightforward success story of the influence of a radical book, or does it show us something else about the relationship between political normality and its opponents? Should we be wary of these concepts making it into parliament, or purely celebratory of the fact?

Capitalist Realism's main intention was to make something clear that was under the surface in both Slavoj Žižek and Frederic Jameson's philosophy: that capitalism and reality have become words with the same meaning, so that thinking of an alternative to capitalism is as hard as thinking of an alternative to reality. On the one hand, it is obviously a good thing to see a radical book, containing a powerful critique of capitalism, have such a big impact that is very much outside of small radical (and often academic) circles. On the other hand, the use of the term in the House of Commons might point us to another danger.

The absorption of the term 'capitalist realism' into mainstream politics and popular political commentary would show something that Fisher himself argued: that capitalist realism survives by turning its opponents into a part of its own logic and language. Fisher's argument is threatening to political discourse, but the absorption of the term 'capitalist realism' into the House of Commons may indicate something other than its success as a radical idea: that it has been dealt with by being made a part of political discourse. On the other hand, another possible outcome here is that McDonnell will stop mentioning radical things, such as Fisher's idea of capitalist realism, as he inhabits a position of greater political power (although the Mao incident discussed above might suggest otherwise). Thankfully, at the moment his and Corbyn's straight-talking appear to be continuing untrammelled, but will this continue if and when these figures become those in actual power? It remains to be seen.

Fisher's book (despite its success) remains in the quite radical position of being outside the norms of journalism and political culture. In fact, it might be influential in forming a new community outside of the established (and very capitalist) ones. However, Fisher's argument also asks us to be attentive to the way that capitalism absorbs its enemies by turning them into something that makes sense in its own terms. Capitalism *rationalises*, glossing over the radicalism in its opponents, and making them a part of its own discourse. With Fisher's idea of 'capitalist realism' spreading through social media and the left-wing press, it had to be 'acknowledged'. But what role will this acknowledgement play? Will it signify the final success of the book, testifying to the fact that it has really infiltrated politics from outside and opened up discussion? Or will it signify the end of its success, the fact that yet again capitalism has been able to absorb its opponent into its own framework?

Supporters of our current left-wing politicians though we are, can we really feel this reference to 'capitalist realism' will mean we are dealing with a politics that is not separate from but a part of the left-wing blogosphere and its social media, that is connected to the literary radical? Indeed, do we want to erase this gap? Probably there is no clear answer to this question, but we must be attentive to the *politics* of something appearing to be part of politics, and how this re-writes and re-inscribes the line between the political mainstream and the radical voices kept out of it. Their merger, however, could be the bearing of what we call a 'politactics'...

c)

As the preceding articles make clear, one of the key battlefields within British Politics over the next four years, and beyond, will be over the meaning of Jeremy Corbyn. Ironically for someone who consistently rejects personal slurs and *ad hominem* attacks, and who chooses to act as a mouthpiece for others during Prime Minister's Questions, it is what Corbyn himself signifies that is currently, and is likely to remain, in question. Is he a terrorist-sympathiser or the voice of the people? Does he represent the past or the future?

Is it too cynical to suspect that the cultivation of such confusion is exactly what those in power are counting upon? In the dying years of the Cold War, Guy Debord described how 'disinformation' had become a tool by which the dominant society defended itself from criticism. Whatever threatens dominant (i.e. spectacular) society is portrayed as obscure, unclear, a source of confusion. In this case it is not necessary to debunk the particular claims or policies put forward by someone like Corbyn; it is enough to establish a level of uncertainty around what he represents, so that the status quo appears by comparison a source of security and certainty. This is a defensive measure. As Debord puts it, 'the concept of disinformation is only valid for counter-attack. It must be kept in reserve, then rapidly thrown into the fray to drive back any truth which has managed to get through.'[74] There are risks to such a tactic however. On the one hand, it cannot be indefinitely sustained, and on the other, the public may come to recognise that the source of disinformation is not Corbyn but those who fear him as a threat.

4

In the Divided Kingdom

What Happens When Something Fascist Happens? What the Queen's Nazi Salute Shows Us

A video has emerged from 1933/4 showing the seven-year-old queen raising her hand in a Nazi salute along with her mother and her uncle, who would go on to become King Edward VIII. The *Sun*, who uncovered the video, made a point of focusing their criticism away from the young queen and onto her uncle, a man who has a history of Nazi-sympathising and is certainly more deserving of criticism than a playful child copying her mother. However, all the headlines unsurprisingly focus on the queen herself, and it's difficult to imagine that this level of media and public shock would have met the emergence of the video had she not been present at the ill-fated salute. The media is awash with comment on the subject, debating whether or not the paper was 'right' to publish the material, but no one has noted the importance of the timing of this video and no one has assessed the public and the media's almost paranoiac reaction to seeing the footage, both of which tell us important truths about our particular contemporary moment.

It is fairly evident and well documented by the Left that nationalism and patriotism have risen to another wave of prominence in our ideology over the past five years, not so much with the recent attempt to dismiss the SNP, on account of their nationalism, but as a result of the political agenda of our own government, who have systematically placed a focus on 'British tradition' since they came to power in 2010. In that time the British Olympics, the Diamond Jubilee, the Royal Wedding and the birth of two royal babies have been culturally central, whilst anti-European policy is back on the table in the House of Commons and in political media discourse.

Žižek has written that people can respond to capitalism and its global and universal scope by resorting to 'paranoiac overidentification' with people, things, or concepts.[75] In other words, the more capitalism tends to universalise and bring everything and everyone into its scope, the more we seek identification with things that will group as unique identities, the more we might reach for something like nationalism.

It is into a moment characterized by this overidentification with Britishness (the dangers of which are testified to by UKIP and by several dangerous Tory policies) that this Nazi-salute video emerges. This makes its emergence shocking for several reasons. First, it reminds us that we are very much part of a European history and that whilst we try to distance ourselves from any involvement in fascism, there may be parts of our history and our present that are not as far from these dangerous ideologies as we like to think. Many contemporary attitudes towards immigration and Europe testify to this. Second, the footage reminds us of what nationalism and patriotism can lead to, making it a very unwelcome reminder for those politicians and media outlets looking to harness patriotic attitudes to sell their own agendas.

The family setting of the video may make it doubly unsettling; in some way it mirrors the images in the papers over the last few weeks of the perfect royal nuclear family of William and Kate. Whilst that family embodies the Britishness with which we are supposed to identify, this footage shows a child with her mother and controversial uncle, an unusual combination making a controversial and unusual gesture. It provides a timely reminder of the dangers of overidentification and of the path that patriotism can take us down, and operates as a thorn in the side of those who want to encourage us to identify with each other through images of Britishness; hence the instant paranoid reactions of both the Palace and the BBC.

Hegemony and Scottish Independence Strategy: Towards a Radical Democratic Politics

Commiserations to the people of Scotland. The ironic doppelgänger of that big word 'Independence' that will flash like a painful strobe light when UKIP cut deeper into the political landscape of this undeniably *divided* kingdom next year (that is, in the 2015 General Election) will no doubt be a bitter and cruel pill to have to swallow. Whilst the queen will have been left happy that the care of the grounds of her holiday home will still be in the hands of her subjects, the 'historic event' of the referendum – as it will be endlessly called by the BBC (through the skin of their smirking teeth) – has narrowly missed its eventality, which must now remain latent in it.

Like in the case of Ireland, nationalism is a different word for Scotland than for England and the Britain that believes itself to be 'great'. For the latter, the word carries so many overtones of *imperialism*, which – the empire having lost its burly and uncompromising might – now finds its most concentrated dilution in the consciousness of defence leagues and bloody nasty people fighting (imaginary wars) on the national front. For the former, however, it has to do with a recent history of exploitation without proper political representation, such as in Thatcher's trial of the poll tax, or in the determination of the Tory party to retain the union for its own financial benefit, and to govern Scotland despite the fact that the Tories have no chance of being elected there. Indeed, Ireland's centuries-long oppression was at the hands of an imperial Britain that hated it as much under republican as under monarchical rule. The situation is of course not the same in Scotland; the country is not militarily controlled by the English, nor are its national identifiers and pastimes banned, as Ireland's were, but its main government – the government that its government ultimately has to answer to – is that of the United Kingdom as a whole, run by the Conservatives (the Lib Dems' input into the so-called coalition not quite scratching the surface of being even tokenistic), which a quick glance at the 2010 General Election results will show is in no way representative of Scotland's political outlook. With an exception that proves the rule Tory blue stops before the border on the map of that election's results.

As Kunal Modi put it: 'for the first time in the life of any UK national under 40, [this] referendum offer[ed] a real, tangible alternative to the centrist monotony of politics as dictated from on high by the moon-faced neoliberal twat parade currently housed in Westminster'.[76] Indeed, it was not only the idea of independence, but the referendum itself that offered a real, tangible alternative. The panic of the three main parties – bound in a tightknit hegemony – scurrying to make concessions to Scotland in the days running up to the referendum are testament to the referendum itself disrupting the usual order of political discourse. In the philosopher Jacques Rancière's terms, the referendum shifted the 'distribution of the sensible'; that is, the way that the discourse of power allots perceivable, fixed places to political entities.[77] In the run-up to the referendum, these co-ordinates were disrupted. Scotland itself was no longer situated in a place comfortable to power, and moreover, the people themselves suddenly became a different political force: everybody knew the turnout would be high, and that many more young people (including 16 and 17 year-olds) would be voting. It is true that the SNP were leading the Yes campaign, but this was no guarantee of an SNP government after independence. Indeed, much of what was so exciting about the prospect of a Yes vote was the total unknowability of what might have come after. It was likely, of course, to be another liberal parliamentary democracy (though one markedly more equitable, socially democratic and less warmongering than the one Scotland is now stuck with), but such was the intense engagement here in politics that other political formations – based on such widespread direct engagement with democracy – became potentially possible.

It was in the face of a much wider, more truly democratic politics that the three main parties had to make such huge concessions. They had to pay lip service to this truly democratic possibility in order to close it down. Sadly it seems to have worked. There is no guarantee that their 'vow' will be upheld (both the Tories and the Lib Dems have broken major, abstract promises they made before the General Election). This vow, even as it stands, ensures that the new distribution of the *sensible* will be returned to its previous co-ordinates. The vow ensures the continuation of liberal parliamentary democracy, ultimately controlled by Westminster.

The challenge now then is to ensure that the new political subjectivisation and new political experiences of the Scottish people remain open, that the co-ordinates remain redistributed, outside of the authority of the political elite. Even with a No vote this moment of democracy can be kept open precisely because the people as a whole engaged in it. If that political engagement can be sustained, then the discourse of politicians – now held much more directly to account – must also have to radically alter. The redistribution of the sensible *can* alter politics just as much as nations and peoples. This will be a hard task though. Already the media, the government and big business are moving to restore the old order of things. We are immediately told that this No vote was justified because it has stabilised markets. The message here is ultimately, as it is perennially: 'don't get too democratic in future because the markets might crash'!

Reading the British Passport

In 2010 the British Passport was redesigned. While the front cover retained its familiar burgundy colour and UK coat of arms, the interior pages saw a subtle but significant change. Whereas the previous version had identical patterns on each page, with a simple watermark featuring the four national plants of the United Kingdom (rose, thistle, leek and shamrock), the new version features a series of images of landscapes from across the UK, accompanied by various weather symbols (rainclouds, snowclouds, cold fronts etc. – a comment perhaps on the British fascination with the weather). These images are not foregrounded, however, since each page is also blank, ready to be stamped by border staff. Instead, they fade into the background, an underlying, barely registered presence in every new passport.

With this change, the British passport, one of the country's most important and recognisable symbols of national identity, has come to materially signify the way national identity is ideologically established and maintained. Ideology functions as a background to our everyday life, something that does not (seem to) interfere with our actions, as these images do not interfere with the passport's ability to function as a travel document. What happens, though, if these images are brought into the foreground? What, for a start, do they actually depict?

All are real sites from around the UK, such as the White Cliffs of Dover, but the Passport Authority has also included generic descriptions of the pictures on the left-hand edge of each page. From front to back, these are as follows:

- Reedbed
- Geological Formation
- Coastal Cliff
- Fishing Village
- Beach
- Canal
- Village Green
- Formal Park
- Woodland
- Lake

- River
- Moorland
- Mountain

There seems to be a coastal slant here, especially in the first five items (the 'geological formation' is Giants Causeway in Northern Ireland, a coastal feature), representing, perhaps, the passport's role in border crossing, and conversely in securing national borders, which are in the UK contiguous (except in Ireland) with the coastline. Yet as the list continues, this is no longer the case. We enter a pastoral world of natural features: lake, river, moorland and mountain. Again, though, not every item on the list is a natural feature. Perhaps the most telling images are grouped in the middle of the passport: the canal, village green and formal park. Along with the fishing village, these are man-made features of the landscape, but of a very particular kind. All stand for a traditional vision of rural, safe, monocultural, conservative, picturesque Britishness, or even Englishness. If this list is supposed to represent the UK, then it is strikingly biased. There are no city features here, not even any towns. It is not representative of Britain as it is, but of a certain dream of Britain; one that is resolutely anti-modern.

Most significant of all, though, is that not one page of the passport includes an image of a person. Even on the village green, the park bench stands empty. Despite this, the passport can be racially characterised, and characterised as white. Whiteness is, in the West, the race that is not seen, since it is always seen as natural and normal. Whiteness is the default race, the background. By failing to include images of people, the passport occludes the fact that none of the places it depicts are associated with immigrant groups. Formal parks, fishing villages and canals are not just rural locations, they are also, overwhelmingly, white locations. Moreover, the absence of people (the people who actually make up the nation) suggests the passport's primary purpose, which is not to bring people into the nation, but to exclude them. These pristine images of rural Britain paint an idealised picture of an unpopulated country, one that has been protected from uncontrolled immigration of those people who lack such passports.

Another recent change to the British passport seems to stand in stark opposition to these images of rural utopia: the introduction of biometric computer chips, included in passports since 2006. Biometric chips signify a high-tech, modern world, consisting of computerised data and automated checking procedures. This world of advanced security could not be further away from the moorlands and mountains depicted inside the passport. Yet, taken as a total object, the passport tells us that these two things are intimately connected. If we want to have our rural, utopian Britain, we must also accept an increasingly greater emphasis on, and empowerment of, the nation's security apparatus. The traditional rural landscape of the nation (which is always, of course, a myth), can only be sustained – and sustained as ideology – by that which is most modern. The introduction of rural images in the new British passport is not, then, in opposition to biometric technology, but intimately bound up with it, as its almost invisible ideological underpinning and justification.

The Campaign for Nuclear War and the Unknown Known

As Slavoj Žižek explains: 'in March 2003, Donald Rumsfeld' – a man whose finger was never too far from the button – 'engaged in a little amateur philosophizing about the relationship between the known and the unknown: "There are known knowns. These are things we know that we know. There are known unknowns. That is to say, there are things that we know we don't know. But there are also unknown unknowns. There are things we don't know we don't know."'[78] Žižek then fills in the remaining gap: 'what he forgot to add was the crucial fourth term: the "unknown knowns," things we don't know that we know, which is precisely the Freudian unconscious, the "knowledge that doesn't know itself," as Lacan used to say'.

The criticism that Jeremy Corbyn has met with for the fact that he would not be prepared to launch a nuclear bomb or two should things get a bit hairy (tantamount in itself to something of a campaign *for* nuclear war, or at least for Cold War II) might wish to categorise itself, should it have to, under the 'known unknown' – or even 'unknown unknown' – tag.[79] That is, the arguments might run along the lines of: 'we know there are a lot of baddies in the world, but we don't know what they're capable of', in the first instance; or even, 'we'll never know what might be round the corner, so it's best to arm ourselves to the teeth', in the second – in support of a 'nuclear deterrent' (any launch of which would expose the oxymoron that the concept is supposedly based on). However, these logics seem to be operating in the mode of disavowal, specifically in relation to the latter clause in each (and the former too, in the second): the 'unknown'. That is, what is truly radical – perhaps even terrifying – about the unknown is its contentlessness. The 'known unknown' argument of 'there are things we know we don't know, which we have to protect ourselves against with a nuclear deterrent', elides this precise emptiness. The unknown is not actually known here, but knowledge of it is *assumed*, a form of knowledge generally agreed upon as rather reckless. It is the same in the case of the unknown unknown, except doubled (the liminal point of the unknown cannot in fact be accessed, as Kant might have argued).[80] In both, the radical aspect of the contentlessness of the unknown is disavowed: 'I know very well that I don't know, but nevertheless I assume I do know'. These, then, should rather be categorised under the 'unknown known'. The unknown known, that is, of an *assumptive* unconscious.

What this continual assumption will lead to – or we could even say, what it has been creative of, in the stagnation and stalemate of the Cold War and what's followed – is the type of paranoiac state recounted in *The WikiLeaks Files*, that 'Daniel Ellsberg—later famous for leaking the Pentagon Papers—[and who] had a top-secret security clearance' warned Henry Kissinger of:

[I]t will… become very hard for you to learn from anybody who doesn't have these clearances. Because you'll be thinking as you listen to them: "What would this man be telling me if he knew what I know? Would he be giving me the same advice, or would it totally change his predictions and recommendations?" You will deal with a person who doesn't have those clearances only from the point of view of what you want him to believe and what impression you want him to go away with, since you'll have to lie carefully to him about what you know. In effect, you will have to manipulate him. You'll give up trying to assess what he has to say. The danger is, you'll become something like a moron. You'll become incapable of learning from most people in the world, no matter how much experience they may have in their particular area that may be greater than yours.[81]

Firstly, perhaps we should recognise that Corbyn is in effect someone without these 'clearances' – currently – that we (and those that do have them) might in fact be able to learn something from, should we (and they) not let the content of the clearances get in the way. But secondly, what we see here is that the content of the clearance is in fact contentlessness itself; what is in exchange in the paranoid economy laid out above is not the knowledge that this person with access to it has, but rather the non-knowledge that those without access to it represent. It is on this contentlessness that the former speculates: to every response, he must ask: 'but would that response be the same if they knew what I know?' A question which – whether the answer is, 'yes, the response would be the same', or no – could only really lead to dictatorially tying itself up in solipsistic knots.

The unconscious of the assumptive 'unknown known' would thus lead to action being taken based upon inklings and hunches, such as was the case in the war with Iraq – which was started through suspicion that Saddam Hussein possessed Weapons of Mass Destruction – Bush and Blair's disavowal of which operated in the mode of: 'I know very well that all the reconnaissance suggests he hasn't, but all the same...'

So much of today's international situation is a result of such an assumption; how much of tomorrow's do we want to be? Those calling on Corbyn to (be prepared to) push the button should perhaps put themselves forward for election to the task of doing so, for if they truly wish to raise the unknown known of such an action to the known known of nuclear devastation – that is, to 'become Death, the destroyer of worlds', in J. Robert Oppenheimer's words, taken from the *Bhagavad Gita*; to fight World War III with the weapons that would insist that World War IV is fought with sticks and stones, as Albert Einstein put it – then this would represent the ethics of, to coin a phrase, an *unconscience* from which what we could learn not only is already known to us, but, should its result come about, would force (once again, after Hiroshima and Nagasaki) the utter radicality of the contentlessness of the unknown unknown into reality itself.

5

States of Nations, and Nationalist States

The Kanye West Wing and the Rise of the Entertainment State

At the VMA awards in August 2015, Kanye West took to the stage to accept his Video Vanguard Award from Taylor Swift. He concluded his acceptance speech by announcing that he would be running for President of the United States. The audience, consisting of multi-millionaires, bestselling musicians and mega celebrities, all cheered and fist-pumped in approval. Those who saw the event on television, and were all-too used to West's proclamations and stage-hogging antics, assumed it was a lark. The following month, West's statement drew remarks from President Barack Obama. Obama offered the mock-advice to West: 'you got to deal with strange characters who behave as if they are on a reality TV show', a reference to West's wife, reality-television star and possible future First Lady, Kim Kardashian. He then continued: 'do you really think this country is going to elect a black guy from the southside of Chicago with a funny name to be president of the US?'[82] Of course... stranger things have happened, are happening, and are yet to occur in America.

To be clear, this is not to dismiss West as a presidential contender. In another life he might make an outstanding public servant. In some respects, West's upbringing and background would even prepare him for public office. From a young age he showed a proficiency for art and eventually became involved in Chicago's vibrant hip-hop scene, first as a writer and producer, then morphing into a world-class performer. West carries more weight as a Man-of-the-People figure than even Obama can muster. Certainly he is more connected to the plights, triumphs and failings of modern Americans than, say, current Republican candidate Donald Trump. In 2005, when West appeared in a live telethon in support of the victims of Hurricane Katrina, he proclaimed to the audience that 'George Bush does not care about black people', which summed up the feelings of frustration against the Bush administration.[83] As the situation played out in New Orleans, one could hardly disagree with West's comments. West has also shown divergence from popular discourse. Before his presidential announcement he even suggested some pretty radical amendments to popular culture:

I believe in myself, we the Millennials bro. This is a new mentality. We not gonna control our kids with brands. We're not going to teach low self esteem and hate to our kids. We're going to teach our kids that they can be someone. We're going to teach our kids that they can stand up for themselves. We're going to teach our kids to believe in themselves. It's about ideas, new ideas, people with ideas, people who believe in truth.[84]

At worst, West's ambitions point towards something more sinister: the belief that politicians should be suave, savvy, well-chiselled iconoclasts with easy soundbites and a digestible platform, as opposed to being hard-working lawmakers who understand the hardships people face. We are venturing further towards an age of extreme spectacle, where reality and fantasy converge. The ascent of Donald Trump's campaign for the 2016 Republican Party nomination has shown that Americans may even be prepared for such spectacle to occur. Trump's approach has been to tap into the extreme prejudices against immigration that lie within the dark heart of the American psyche, and to blame immigration on the financial and cultural wasteland that is apparently rampant. Trump's answers are extreme: build real walls to keep immigrants out, build virtual walls to keep prejudice locked in. Trump's merciless nature and desire for conflict is extremely dangerous in a world faced with tremendous unrest. Nonetheless, at the time of writing, Trump has excelled in the opinion polls.

As detestable as it sounds, Donald Trump and Kanye West are reading from a similar script. Like Trump, West's positions on matters such as medical care, US foreign policy, finance, economics, care for the elderly and poor, America's space program and education reform have not been disclosed. If West's campaign is real, he will have to work with a huge group of managers, organisers and volunteers, and here lies the problem. There is a false presumption in America that the presidency is the ultimate accumulation of power and status, the totality of the American Dream. But the presidency is far more than just one individual. There is a cabinet office, a senate, the people to contend with. Based on his evocations of Christ-like imagery (e.g. in the song 'I am a God' from an album called *Yeesus*), the vision West has for his presidency will be to embody every aspect of America. With lack of experience in representing real Americans, this embodiment of every American reality is ultimately an empty vessel, and makes any post-Kanye presidency seem worthless, with any popularity-seeker vying for office (Lindsey Lohan stated she'd run in 2010) and willing to flip the switch from self-involved to righteous.

In his 2009 book, *Empire of Illusion: The End of Literacy and the Triumph of Spectacle*, Chris Hedges applies commentary to the mass disillusion that America seems to be partaking of. Hedges comments that 'the worse reality becomes, the less a beleaguered population wants to hear about it, and the more it distracts itself with squalid pseudo-events of celebrity breakdowns, gossip, and trivia'.[85] The pseudo-events and trivialities have now entered into the political playing-field. Under this cardboard template of democracy the atrocities of rampant capitalism, the crippling of the working classes, the decimation of the environment, the failings of the education system can continue unabated, and Kanye West would be powerless to stop it, even if he wanted to. After all, his presidency is just another tick-off in his path to popularity, as he said at the VMAs: 'I just want people to like me!' A West Presidency would be trading record sales and ticket stubs for votes. No longer will America exist in the same reality as the rest of the world. America will instead operate in a permanent state of entertainment. No lefty, moderate or right-winger with hard-earned credentials will dare to follow the circus.

a)

The above article points out – in relation to Trump, who is thundering away in the race for the Republican presidential candidacy – that, despite his dangers, he is excelling in the polls. Where this view perhaps stops short is in seemingly *universalising* a form of rationality that is perceptive of these dangers; that is, in making it into a 'common sense' supposedly common to all, building a further sense that 'Trump's comments and sentiments won't fly with the enlightened mainstream'.

However, fascism, just because defeated once – and despite this defeat's continued celebration – doesn't mean it can't rear its ugly head on a grand scale again, if conditions are right. Where its material realisations are to be found in the Trump phenomenon is in a certain vigilantism that has been condoned through his meteoric rise and the free rein of his speech. At his rallies, attestations of the increasing violence against attending protestors and journalists are rife, prejudicial, discriminatory comments are commonly heard uttered by crowd members, and racism and sexism, spewed from the stage, is echoed by his supporters, as if they're finally getting the sanction of the state that they've always been waiting for.[86]

Although – emphatically – *not* the president, Trump appears to his supporters as an establishment figure, using a language powerful and seemingly incumbent enough to give free rein to the dangerous desires and delusions of the hardcore Trump-faithful; although – emphatically – *not* a lawmaker, his words are becoming vigilante law to those citizens who take it into their heads that because a prominent figure is saying such things, posters can be put up in grocery stores or carparks indicating 'Muslim-free zones', for example.[87] This hate speech, trumpeted by Trump, is beginning to create a vigilantism not dissimilar to that of the street anti-gay groups in Russia who took its law into their own hands, by seeing in what has been allowed in speech and rhetoric the passage to material transubstantiation: words turning into actions.[88] This entails a dark precursor that we must remain wary of.

On Peshawar

On 16 December 2014 armed gunmen broke into a school killing at least 132 people and injuring many more. Almost exactly two years earlier, on 14 December 2012, a lone gunman entered another school, in another country, killing 26 people and leaving many others with life-altering injuries. The scale of these attacks is almost irrelevant; both are utterly tragic massacres of innocent people in a school, a place where they should feel safe. Both of these events should demand world attention, supporting the communities in coming to terms with the trauma that has occurred, working with governments to do everything possible to ensure that murder on this scale, in this manner, never happens again.

The day after the Sandy Hook shooting at an elementary school in America, eleven of twelve main UK newspapers reported the event on their front pages.[89] Calls of outrage about what had happened alternated with pictures and naming of the deceased. The coverage was designed to pull at the heartstrings: articles talked of families who would be without their loved ones at Christmas. These were real people everyone could relate to, these were people's children who had died. The coverage did not stop there; the following day seven newspapers reported the story on their front pages and a week later, despite it being the height of the Christmas season, two newspapers featured Sandy Hook on their front pages. The story did not die away completely for several weeks.

Contrast this then with the massacre of schoolchildren in Peshawar, Pakistan, by Taliban militants. The following day this story was featured on the front page of eight national newspapers, and in only one of these was it the only feature on the page.[90] Now why is this? Neither of these events happened in the UK. They both happened thousands of miles away, they are both unquestionably tragic. And yet, 132 people, many of them children, were killed in Peshawar and in the British media only eight of the national newspapers even ran this as a front-page story. Why do we report these two events vastly differently? Do we put a higher price on the life of children in Sandy Hook because we can relate to them more easily than over 100 Muslim children in Pakistan? And if the answer to that is yes, surely we need to ask ourselves some searching questions about what it says about us as a society, and about valuations of life on a global scale.

It's not just in the media that this divide is apparent. Contrast too the comments of David Cameron. In relation to Sandy Hook, he said: 'my thoughts are with those who have been devastated by the Sandy Hook shootings'.[91] On Peshawar, he comments: 'it's horrifying that children are being killed simply for going to school'.[92] Look at the marked difference in the emotion displayed here. To the first he instantly relates, to the second it's a much more objective comment about children's right to go to school. Barack Obama, so obviously personally touched by what happened in Sandy Hook, speaks only of America's desire to stand with Pakistan over the latest atrocity. 'We reiterate the commitment of the United States to support the government of Pakistan in its efforts to combat terrorism and extremism and to promote peace and stability in the region.'[93] The personal touch seems strangely missing.

Emotions aside, the consequences of the Peshawar shooting are likely to be devastating in a country where education, for girls in particular, is a constant struggle. With so many schoolchildren recently murdered, the campaign for girls' education in Pakistan – led so eloquently by Malala Yousafzai – is in grave danger of facing massive setbacks, if it does not become derailed altogether. This is a time when newspapers, politicians and anybody with a voice that can be heard should be rallying together to shout as loudly as possible about the atrocity that happened in Pakistan, doing everything possible to ensure that children, regardless of race, religion or nationality, can go to school free from fear.

a)

It is, at the time of writing, almost a year since gunmen broke into the Army Public School in the northwestern Pakistani city of Peshawar. They killed 141 people, 132 of them schoolchildren between eight and eighteen years of age. This was the deadliest terrorist attack ever to occur in Pakistan.

At the time international response to the shooting felt muted and, as discussed in the article above, there was a huge disparity in coverage between Peshawar and the American school shooting in 2012 at Sandy Hook, in which 26 people were fatally shot. Coverage of the Peshawar massacre lasted barely two days before it faded from media interest, leaving behind a broken school in an area where children, particularly girls, have always had to fight to even be allowed to go to school.

This was a time for commentators and journalists in the West to stand up and unite in the fight; a time to join inspirational campaigners such as Malala Yousafzai in declaiming how terrible it is that children are not able to gain an education, a basic children's right, in safety. A Google News search on the subject brings up only small articles from Asian newspapers over the past year reporting other terrorist threats to schools and a few articles about the investigation. It is hard to find anything on the subject from well-known Western publications. It seems the aftermath of such an event in Pakistan is not worth reporting. By contrast, three years on, a search for Sandy Hook still brings up a multitude of follow-up articles from a huge range of sources.

A year on, schooling, particularly for girls, is still under threat. Peshawar and the constant threat of similar attacks scare parents into keeping their children at home. It's an incredibly difficult situation and one that has been made far more difficult by what happened last December. It takes brave, determined people to stand up against the Taliban as the consequences for opposing them can be fatal. One such group, 'Aware Girls', a network of young, female activists who peacefully oppose the Taliban, is based in Peshawar.[94] They are firm in their belief that the best way to beat terrorism is by educating people, speaking with young people and showing them that there are ways out of terrorism. It's a message that surely needs to be spread, not just throughout Pakistan, but far beyond. Organisations such as this deserve, and need, publicity. Getting support for people who are advocating for equality in education, trying to show people another way, is how things are going to change for the people of Peshawar. One way this could happen is if causes such as this were more widely reported and a small group of women given support from larger, more powerful organisations. This is unlikely to happen when the media seem largely to have forgotten what happened in Peshawar.

On ISIS

November 13 2015 will probably be remembered for a long time for the atrocity carried out by terrorists in the city of Paris. 132 ordinary people were killed, going to a concert, eating at a restaurant and doing the kinds of ordinary things we do without a second thought for our safety and security.

ISIS are beginning to change that. A terrorist group, with barbaric and evil intent, are starting to make cities feel unsafe. This is, of course, a situation that cannot be allowed to continue. We cannot get to a point where people cannot go to work, cannot go for dinner or to concerts for fear of what might happen. We cannot let suicide bombers dictate whether events can take place; doing that is letting them gain a victory through their atrocious actions. Governments and political leaders have got to take the anger generated by the Paris attack, and the Russian aeroplane attack, and the Tunisian beach attack, and the multitude of other ISIS attacks across the world, and use it to do something powerful to stop them.

Keen to take decisive action, several countries have begun air strikes over ISIS locations in Syria and it seems likely Britain will soon join them. Understandably, leaders want to be seen do be doing something, and force is a powerful way of showing that. But this is not simply a case of declaring war; what, exactly are we 'going to war' with? ISIS are not a simply tangible force; this isn't declaring war on a country, it is attempting to fight an amorphous, sometimes invisible group who hide in places that are not easily reachable. The effects of such a war could be devastating, not only because they are likely to be unsuccessful, but because of the long-term damage such a war could do to innocent Muslim people across the world.

Muslims are not terrorists, Muslims died in Paris, Muslims regularly speak out against the horrors of ISIS and yet warmongering politicians are already speaking of setting up 'Muslim databases' and setting up surveillance of mosques. These kinds of racist attitudes stir up divisive feelings in communities rather than bringing all the sections of the community to unite against the common enemy. ISIS are not remotely representative of what ordinary Muslim people believe in any way and that message needs to come through loud and clear in the media and from senior politicians.

ISIS thrive on recruiting people from across the world to go to Syria and Iraq and join their cause. Rather than singling out and isolating Muslim communities, we should be promoting better education here. We should teach in schools what the Muslim religion is about, so that people grow up with an understanding that it is fundamentally peaceful. Politicians, leaders in mosques, teachers in schools, should talk loudly and publically about why ISIS does not represent Islam. The media should dedicate time and space to promoting this message so that Muslim people can continue to feel and to be an integral part of society. With better education the 'Islamic State' may begin to become less appealing to young people. For those determined to go, border security needs to be tougher. For countries so concerned about immigration, perhaps we need to look more closely at emigration, ensuring that people who could be headed for ISIS are stopped before they have the chance to get there. Fewer people reaching Syria leaves fewer people to be trained for the purposes for which ISIS plans to use them.

ISIS cannot generate their weapons and staff their terror camps without money and governments should be targeting the sources of their income and cutting it off immediately. The group control several oil wells in Iraq and Syria which export oil to neighbouring countries. Surely there is space here for diplomatic negotiations with these countries to stop them paying ISIS for supplies. This would drastically reduce their available funds and make it difficult for them to procure more sophisticated, deadlier weapons. Working in coalition with leaders of other Arab countries may also bring about further information about the locations of the leaders of ISIS so that if military intervention happened it would be targeted, focused on clearly identified locations, with clear targets in mind.

It is without doubt that ISIS need be stopped, so that people can go about their lives without fear of attack and persecution. Rather than embarking on a long, dangerous war without any clearly defined aim, we should instead be concentrating on uniting our communities and making them safe places for people of all races to live in and putting our efforts into halting ISIS recruitment, whilst cutting off their financial supplies, so that they lose the tools and the conditions that they need to thrive.

Beauty and the Beast: #CeciltheLion and the 'Migrants'

One of the biggest-trending Twitter hashtags recently has been '#CeciltheLion'. The killing of a lion by a rich American has stimulated outpourings of anger, disgust and sadness. The reporting of the story has run in conjunction with a really shocking event: 'migrants' in Calais are dying in an attempt to reach British shores in the hope of a better life. As pointed out in a number of articles in the *Independent* and the *Guardian*, these migrants are afforded nowhere near the same degree of compassion or empathy as 'Cecil'. A *New Statesman* article on the subject picks up on the importance of the language used by politicians, celebrities and media in describing the two news stories.[95] What is argued here is that the language used in these two cases shows us that there is something increasingly proto-fascist about the political, and social, establishment at the moment, something a recent Everyday Analysis article suggested in a different context.[96]

As a result of having been endowed with the name of 'Cecil', the lion has been humanised. As with our pets, the lion's name includes it as one of the human family (which perhaps explains why the lion was given a British imperialistic name instead of one that originates from Zimbabwe). The name automatically conveys his belonging and acceptance, he is 'one of us', a 'member of the family'. Just a few hours ago the *Daily Mail* reported that Cecil's brother 'Jericho' may also have been killed by poachers after earlier reporting that Jericho was looking after Cecil's cubs for him.[97] This very comically shows us that we relate to these animals as 'one of us', even as if they share our family values.

Whilst 'Cecil' has been *humanised*, thousands of 'migrants' have at the same time been *dehumanised* by the right-wing press and even, perhaps unsurprisingly, by David Cameron. Primarily, the word 'migrant' used to describe the people in Calais points us away from thinking of people as refugees: in the past few decades, people fleeing war-torn countries undergoing complete social decimation have been referred to as 'asylum-seekers', moving towards a haven, safety and the prospect of a new secure life. Now, however, the right-wing press, including the BBC, have ensured that the term 'migrant' has become hegemonic, a word embroiled in the worlds of market and capital, used to suggest that people have made the economic decision to leave their homes to set up in Britain. 'Migrant' also signifies the movements of animals when the weather changes, and this is where the right-wing, proto-fascist process of dehumanising desperate people becomes potent.

Rendered nameless and consistently referred to en masse as 'the migrants', with no personal detail beyond the generalised notion that they are from 'North Africa' or 'the Middle East', it is emphasised that the people at Calais do not belong, that they are not acceptable nor to be accepted, either in France or Britain. Whilst Cecil is a member of the family, the migrants are not.

Many, including Ricky Gervais, Kristen Davis and the head of the Zimbabwe Conservation Taskforce Johnny Rodrigues, have emphasised the 'beauty' of the lion in relation to their own dismay and outrage at the killing that unfolded. The lion is incredibly aesthetically pleasing, with big round eyes, golden fur, a wide symmetrical face and a huge mane. Along with 'beauty', images of the lion conjure up such words as 'majestic' and 'regal', and it is of a male portion of a species that is frequently referred to as the 'king' of the animal *king*dom. The lion and the king have long been associated with one another: from Hercules wearing the pelt of the Nemean to Richard the Lionheart, Narnia's Aslan, and *The Lion King*. (Historically, fascism has also had this focus on the aesthetic, and specifically on the beauty of the regal and majestic.) Walter Palmer had already killed a cheetah, a white rhino and a bear before 'Cecil', but the same level of furore and anger has not surfaced until now. Cecil the lion actually seems to represent the ideas of a regal and majestic centre, a 'beautiful', king-like, powerful figure who represents us and our family and political values, explaining why his death troubles us so much.

On the other hand, the media represent 'migrants' as people who don't belong in 'our family', who do not convey an attractive aesthetic sense of regality and majesty. This animalistic dehumanisation has manifested beyond the word 'migrant' and can be seen in the fascist rhetoric of the *Sun*'s Katie Hopkins referring to the refugees as 'cockroaches', or David Cameron describing them as 'swarms'. Whilst the world rallies around the death of a humanised creature it deems beautiful, the people in Calais fleeing horrific conflict are met with degrading, xenophobic and outright fascist attitudes, evident in the right-wing language that constructs them as pests and parasites who multiply and seek to invade.

Whilst the Cecil story and the reporting of the migrants seem like two separate stories, the celebration of something beautiful (Cecil) in fact works alongside the expulsion or rejection of what is deemed not attractive (the 'migrants') by western right-wing politics. This ideology, which involves celebrating the beauty of our centre and rejecting the ugliness of the other, is fundamentally fascist.

Refugees and the Racism Crisis

'Since I must not all the same allow you to look at the future through rose coloured glasses' – Lacan prophesied in 1972 – 'you should know that what is arising, what one has not yet seen to its final consequences, and which for its part is rooted in the body, in the fraternity of the body, is racism, about which you have yet to hear the last word. Voila!'[98] Here, the body – a locus of 'enjoyment' – is made out to be involved with a rise in racism, and this article will try to argue why this is the case for Lacan.

This was something of an enigmatic ending to his nineteenth seminar, pessimistically entitled *...ou pire* – that is, *...or worse* (whilst *'ou père'* can also be heard in the French) – but one through which much can be explored in today's global climate and in relation to attitudes taken to the crisis in Syria that has caused so many of its inhabitants to seek refuge outside of its borders. It is through this psychoanalytic lens that we might begin to unpack these questions, and through yoking it with other important remarks.

In keeping with Lacan's mention of the body in this respect, Paul Gilroy – writing in the 2002 introduction to his classic study *There Ain't No Black in the Union Jack* – talks of 'those sensitive spots where the body of Britain's post-colonial polity was poorly sutured'.[99] He lists certain ways in which such acne-filled or gangrenous spots have come about; that is, through simulacral cultural phenomena of that now-antiquated moment in time like 'the terrace chant of "two world wars and one World Cup"', which 'sounds increasingly bizarre [as] the memory of World War II has been stretched so thin that it cannot possibly accomplish all the important cultural work it is increasingly relied upon to do'.[100] The sparseness of this cultural memory – which has been spread thinly, sensationalistically and all too triumphantly over 'a long loop via Hollywood' – has led a generation 'to use a cheaply-manufactured surrogate memory of it as the favoured means to find and restore [an] ebbing sense of what it is to be English'. This, Gilroy calls 'devolution and disintegration', phenomena which have 'intensified a nagging uncertainty as to the cultural content of national identity', and yet one which makes the old guard feel that 'the newly-devolved are evidently having a better time'...[101]

Enjoyment is seen clearly here as a political factor, as Žižek might say; specifically, the enjoyment of the Other, or of everybody else: of every other body. This version of enjoyment – what Lacan called '*jouissance*' – is inscribed in or on the body, fraternally shared through recognisability in *body language*. If these remarks may be beginning to seem digressive, let's bring them in relation to a meme about the 'migration' crisis – as its being called – that's been doing the rounds amongst racists on social media: two juxtaposed photographs, one apparently depicting a pair of refugees sat at an outside table adorned with teapots, both black, and smiling; the second a dishevelled white man laying against a wall with a dog, apparently homeless. The caption on the first reads: '"Coming to England is like being reborn..." Muhammad'; the second: 'British ex Servicemen should be housed BEFORE asylum seekers. SHARE if you AGREE!' (Although the racism of this meme is glaringly obvious – reinforced by the lack of any identification, authentication, contextualisation etc. of these images – we'll here discuss how it renders the effect its popularity in certain circles suggests it is having, and leave the debunking of its bullshit in the capable hands of *Vice*.[102])

The contrast of these pictures shows those men in the former as clearly having a better time than the other man in the latter. The claim of the contrast is that the latter's enjoyment – like the mythical jobs of the nationalist imagination – is being stolen by the supposed 'immigrants' of the former picture. This is a well-trodden trope of racism; in terms of the perennial theme of employment, for example – a theme which nonetheless always seems a brand new and current epidemic to the racist imagination – fears of said thievery crop up as early as in the American slave Frederick Douglass's narrative of his life of 1845:

All at once, the white carpenters took off, and said they would not work with free colored workmen. Their reason for this, as alleged, was, that if free colored carpenters were encouraged, they would soon take the trade into their own hands, and poor white men would be thrown out of employment.[103]

Enoch Powell's ruminations on which race is entitled to the right to hold 'the whip hand' over others are a mere extension of the purely prejudicial ill-reasoning of the carpenters. In terms of enjoyment, to give one earlier race-based example, blues parties in the homes of Caribbean immigrants to Britain in the 1960s provided a cause of a confused jealousy over an enjoyment that white neighbours had no part in and thus conspiratorially felt was being had at their expense.

The confusional logic of this kind of thinking is relayed succinctly by the psychoanalyst Richard Klein, in relation to the superego, when he states that 'the superego command gives the subject a right-to-enjoy which is then prohibited by calling for his punishment. The more it commands, the more intense the prohibition, and the more virtuous the subject becomes.'[104] When one's enjoyment is both constituted and interdicted by the superego (that psychical realm that sadistically lays down unachievably strict rules of conduct), its puritanical 'virtue' becomes not only directed against the self, but can turn into a power to be punitively wielded against others, in a direct contradiction of the mantra of 'live and let live'. The subject comes to believe that others still possess this uninhibited right-to-enjoy and becomes both envious of them and determined to close it down in them. As Klein says: 'the morality of power makes desire disappear in favour of the service of goods. Power enjoys itself and gives itself a morality.'[105]

With desire quashed, enjoyment transfers over into power, and its resultant 'morality' then 'polices' those that figure in the odds and ends of events and current affairs that it comes across with a guilty-until-proven-innocent suspicion of others that *do* desire (in the example of refugees, desire to escape from life-threatening situations – a strange thing for a redirected envy to be aimed at!). What the superego denies to itself – enjoyment – it sees invading whenever there's movement out of the ordinary in its peripheral vision. The prohibitive subject then attempts to universalise their subjectivity by making nationality the identifier of their superegoic injunction to exclusivity: this leads to such tautologies as being-British being the supreme British virtue (a virtue which is then seen as under threat). The question is: could international solidarity instead of nationalist exclusivity be universalised, or hegemonised, here? Corbyn's first act as Labour leader suggests that there's at least a hope it can.

If this in part is what has been unconsciously underlying populist and right-wing *Daily Mail*- and *Express*-led reaction (to which David Cameron may claim to be responding, whilst he and the UKIP contingent have been fostering it), it may thus represent a racism that does not yet know itself (though it is no less excusable for that): thus, after the out-and-out racists, secondary flanks of people who would never dream of using the 'N-word', for example, are here readily using others just as pejoratively loaded, and drawing from a surrogate and simulacral storehouse of myth and nonsense to underwrite their opinions (one stocked knowingly and connivingly by the all-out racists).

As Gilroy warned in the aforementioned essay: 'there can be no guarantees against the brutal effects of resurgent Islamophobia'.[106]

Prescient words in 2002; may we just hope that those two terrifying words of Lacan's statement in 1972 – 'final consequences' – might be checked by the required efforts of anti-racism.

A Modern Refugee

A Syrian refugee apparently took a selfie on a decent mobile phone and it was not okay with the right-wing militants of Britain. At the moment a hate-fuelled meme is doing the rounds on social media and it tells us some important truths not only about the frighteningly fascist attitudes towards refugees in our country but also about the role that the refugee is expected to play in the ideology of right-wing Britain.

The horrible meme makes out that fleeing a war zone and the traumas associated with that are not enough to deserve our sympathy if you have a Samsung phone. Possess a symbol of capitalist success and modernity, manage a smile of relief and, in our unforgiving political climate, a traumatised refugee is be deemed a fraud. This article thus asks two questions. First, in the eyes of the British Right, why should a refugee not have a mobile phone? Second, why should a refugee not take a selfie?

The *Independent* have pointed out that one of the first things you'd buy if you were fleeing your home is a smartphone, and that people surprised to see Syrian refugees using them are idiots.[107] The smartphone is a symbol of modernity and the claim of the meme is that if you have already been brought into modernity then you do not require our help. This shows a colonial viewpoint still present in our right wing: they see the West as more modern and civilised and expect the countries from which these refugees come to be backwards and primitive. The oddness in the meme is the fact that it claims these countries are just as modern as us, as if we should only be helping 'backwards' or 'primitive' countries and that people from nations with smartphones would be fine on their own.

If refugees are seen to come from a barbaric and uncivilised world that can be labelled primitive then they come from a world that is not that of modernity and this justifies a diminished responsibility on the part of the UK public and politicians. It *naturalises* the refugees' experience and makes it part of the natural or inevitable 'course of history', a language often used by UK and US politicians, meaning that specific political conditions (which the West is responsible for) are not seen as the reason for trauma and devastation. Modernity is not seen as responsible for devastation but as the saviour from it.

In short, the meme claims that people without a smartphone do need our help because they need bringing into Western modernity: fleeing mud huts and 'backwards' nations is okay, but fleeing modernity throws up all sorts of difficult questions surrounding Britain's foreign policy (which has a direct hand in Syrian air strikes) and confronts us with a need to consider the *cause* of fleeing.

So to the second question: why can a refugee not take a selfie? It is first worth noting that some have suggested this meme may even be photoshopped to include the mobile, and second that it is clearly not a 'selfie', in the terms of our culture, but is more likely to be an attempt to communicate the refugee's safety to her family. Nonetheless, the meme and its circulation show that the idea of a refugee taking a selfie is significant. Selfies in themselves are interesting to discuss in that they hold a contro-versial place even in our own society, they are the absolute symbol of modernity, encompassing all sorts of complex arguments about vanity and identity. Having a sense of the portrayal of oneself does not fit in with the image of a refugee that our right-wing culture likes to consume. A refugee taking a selfie throws into question the way that refugees are typecast within our media. The mainstream media response to young, able men being refugees has been written about in the *Huffington Post*, for example: people, and not just those at Britain First, seem troubled by images of refugees that do not conform to their expectations.

In conclusion, whilst Germany and other European countries opened their borders to help ease the crisis, the British media remained closed and unwelcoming. Thankfully, recent weeks have seen a strong backlash against this and the media have begun to take something of a U-turn in their coverage of the international refugee crisis. This is relief from the militant, right-wing stance on the refugee crisis, which shockingly had become the voice of the mainstream media. However, this meme points us to a possible danger that this U-turn is reserved for only the neediest and most desperate (usually women and children), those who aesthetically appear war-torn and desperate enough and conform to our expectations of what a refugee should look like and how a refugee should behave.

In the end, this meme shows us three things. First, it quite simply and obviously shows how much hateful fascism and racism there is in our society. Second, it shows how these structures are still supported by a colonial ideology that sees the passage to modernity as the natural course of events and does not want to admit that this trauma and devastation is a modern problem that our own brand of modernity is responsible for. Third, it warns us of the danger of our preconceptions and expectations when it comes to refugees and shows us how deeply ingrained in right-wing ideology some of our assumptions may be.

6

On Work and Leisure

Oh, the Precarity! *A Worker's-Eye View*

You finally find a job through an employment agency who seem halfway worthwhile, not like the others who you're convinced advertise fake jobs in their windows to get the punter through the door, and then say: 'sorry, that opportunity's just gone' or is 'fully subscribed for interviews now', and offer you something far inferior, if anything at all (but they've got you and will keep you on their books).[108] The work comes in after the best part of a year unemployed, in which you attended meetings at a Job Centre week-in-week-out for a month, only for them to then send a letter declining your Job Seeker's Allowance due to there having been insufficient National Insurance contributions made on your part in the tax year that they assessed, despite the fact that that year you were a student, and struggling to find regular employment then too, and as such could not claim JSA – which would have assisted with the contributions – due to being a student. You mightn't have been in the most desperate of desperate need – but others *are* – but the catch 22 rather goes to highlight that wide gap (obviously not clearly enough marked, as people are forever falling down it) between the media image of the gratuitous ease with which anyone can trade in work for scrounging off the state and the paltriness of provision epitomised in the response to the inquiry about the refusal of benefit (a more adequate, less *accusative* and patronising term for which would surely be 'assistance'): 'you'll be alright though, you've got a qualification.'

The office of this job in administration – paid at minimum wage by the agency – is located on a floor above a company specialising in private surveillance, whose curtains were rather oddly always open (at least until the day after Corbyn's leadership election, perhaps coincidentally) for passers-by to espy their spying on endless personal Facebook and Twitter accounts, no doubt probing claimants' intimate snaps for that revelatory, indemnifying *smile*, and whose slogan, no kidding, was 'turning suspicion into irrefutable evidence', a conversion rate no doubt motivated by targets and incentivised by bonuses. Settling into the job over the first six or so weeks of the twelve of the temp-to-perm contract with the agency, you start to make a few friends, learn the craft, pick up the systems from the training, and then you get the old mid-shift lay-off by the agency, who are in dispute with the company you're working for, claiming they haven't been paying the agency; the retort being that a fair few of the agency staff they've been providing have been up and leaving after a day's (paid) training, but no work, but 'my name's Paul, and this is between y'all'; that is, this dispute doesn't concern the just-terminated worker, whose been used not even as a bargaining tool, but as a weapon of attrition, whose services have just been revoked, by the agency, to spite the company. The agency contact you with another job for tomorrow picking and packing in a factory double the distance of your previous bike-ride commute – that is, hardly like-for-like – in a pathetic attempt to cover their asses, but one no doubt contractually sound.

The term for the working class today finding themselves increasingly in positions like this one – and each no doubt as idiosyncratic – is 'the precariat'. The word is a conjunction of two terms: 'precarity' – being the precarious state that the working class finds itself in today, in relation to the fragility of agency and temporary work, zero-hour contracts, cuts to, and increases in waiting times for, working tax credits and unemployment benefits etc. – and 'proletariat', the working class itself. Indeed, as Guy Standing defines it:

The precariat can be identified by a distinctive structure of social income, which imparts a vulnerability going well beyond what would be conveyed by the money income received at a particular moment. [...] A feature of the precariat is not the level of money wages or income earned at a particular moment but the lack of community support in terms of need, lack of assured enterprise or state benefits, and lack of private benefits to supplement money earnings. [...] The precariat does not feel part of a solidaristic labour community. This intensifies a sense of alienation and instrumentality in what they have to do. [It] knows that there is no shadow of the future, as there is no future in what they are doing. To be 'out' tomorrow would come as no surprise[;] not all those in the precariat should be regarded as victims. Nevertheless, most will be uncomfortable in their insecurity, without a reasonable prospect of escape.[109]

The ennui that comes with the condition of belonging to the precariat is one being capitalised on by the endless rolling back of workers' rights, in terms of regularity and regulation of working hours, pay and pay gaps, and of the ability to strike, all found at risk in the new junior doctors' contract, for example. Indeed, behind Jeremy Hunt's call for his own version of 'Asiatic modes of production' – he said that Brits must work as hard as the Chinese – lays the deeply sinister agenda of ideological austerity, as much aimed at enforcing the austerity of workers' ideas as it is at cutting material resources to society's most precariously placed.[110]

Letter from a Junior Doctor

I am an A&E trainee doctor. I am intensely proud of working for the NHS. And I work hard. At 7am when your dad has a heart attack in A&E, I will be there trying to resuscitate him, whilst also treating your grandma who has come in unable to breathe because her lung disease has got worse, and your son who has broken his leg and is screaming in pain. At 7am I will be 9 hours into my shift and fatigue will be setting in. I am lucky I only work 10-hour shifts. My colleagues in Acute Medicine work 12-hours. They can work for 12 days in a row if the rota falls that way. I'm not asking for sympathy, I don't think any of us are. We expected these working conditions when we decided to train as doctors. I say it merely to show that junior doctors work hard and we are already working at the limits of our capabilities. And it's not just doctors. The nursing staff, radiologists, receptionists, porters – we all work hard, long hours.

The NHS is struggling. I see the gaps in the rota that we have to cover at the same time as our own work. I see that everyone goes the extra mile, working through breaks and leaving hours late because if they don't stay to take these bloods or review this scan or start this IV, then our patient will have to wait even longer. I see waiting times in clinics. I see theatres having to decide which emergency operation is the 'most urgent'. I see hospital beds full of patients unable to leave because of a lack of social care. I see the NHS stretched to capacity to provide a 5-day full service and emergency care out of hours. I cannot see how, with the same resources, we can provide a safe 7-day full service. The 7-day full NHS that Mr Hunt is adamant he is being forced to introduce following the election (although I would argue the significance of his "mandate") is not possible without extra funding and staffing. I see that we will burn out, make mistakes, and it is our patients who will ultimately suffer. I do not understand the blind insistence for 7 days of full service at all costs. Who benefits if you can have your elective knee replacement on a Saturday, but you have to wait five hours to be reviewed when you develop sepsis on the wards on a Tuesday because there aren't enough doctors to cover both? And the simple truth is – there aren't. By imposing this contract, Hunt will force us to provide unsafe care for our patients. Some doctors won't take this risk and will make the decision to leave the NHS. Others will try to carry on, trying to patch up the holes in this sinking ship. Holes that will cause some patients harm.

This argument isn't about pay. We can't deny as a profession, in compensation for our hard work and unsociable hours, we are paid relatively well. Not as well as certain politicians, I might add. But we trained for years to get to this point. We make life and death decisions daily and that is a heavy responsibility. We put in the hours outside of work – we sit professional exams, teach, do research, do audits, read the latest journal articles, make sure we're up to date with the latest developments in our fields. We come out of five years of university with thousands of pounds of debt. We pay professional fees and GMC membership and course fees. Let me make it clear, we aren't asking for a pay rise. These strikes were not about getting more money. But we aren't going to accept a 30% pay cut either. But the money side of things is not the important issue. What it really comes down to is our profession, ours and the safety of our patients and the future of the NHS. And patient safety will suffer under this imposed contract.

The final sticking point in negotiations was the classification of Saturday as a normal day. Despite what Hunt may spin, doctors already work weekends. And nights. And twilight shifts. Because the NHS is already a 7-day service. But as a matter of principle, it should be acknowledged that Saturday is not a normal working day. It is a weekend. It takes more to give up than Monday to Friday. That's not just true for doctors. Many other professions work weekends and this acknowledgement should stand for them too. People are not automatons, there to serve 'industry' or 'capitalism' or a 'system'. They are individuals with lives, with families, and that is just as important a part of life as a career. That is the objection many of us have with the redefinition of Saturday. It is a move to change our cultural thinking and norms. And those who work unsociable hours should be compensated to acknowledge that sacrifice. This isn't about doctors demanding unseemly sums to work weekends. The BMA put forward a cost-neutral proposal that maintained the unsocial hours premium but reduced basic pay-rise to account for that. It was rejected. Mr Hunt has other reasons to push for his Saturday re-brand. Perhaps the upcoming renegotiation of the Nurses contract is on his mind?

Finally, I am so angry. This contract marks a statement of intent. Patient safety no longer comes first, the NHS as we know it is being irrevocably transformed. In the process of sticking the knife into the struggling NHS, Hunt has managed to alienate an entire workforce of junior doctors, riding roughshod over our concerns about patient safety, spreading misinformation and faulty statistics to demonise us and scare our patients, and ultimately imposing a new contract which ethically we cannot comply with. He alienates my profession and good doctors will leave because the working conditions are terrible and there is no prospect of them improving. This is my NHS. I believe passion-ately in it, and I feel powerless to stop its demise. This is why doctors are up in arms.

Modern Work, Modern Play

Take on the Twisters is the latest ITV dinnertime game show repre-sentative of a trend in mainstream modern play of emulating modern work. Its rules subject its contestants at various points to the element of *chance*, an increasingly popular technique in TV gaming that has begun to replace the level-playing-field format of questions and answers (from which contestants answering correctly gain qualification or victory) or set tasks (in which players can outdo each other to win, à la *15 to 1*, *Countdown*, et al). Throughout this game's stages risks loom chancily and threaten-ingly, but in its showdown – the 'final twist' – the real chance element comes in: the contestant at the end must try to keep as many 'twisters' – coloured discs with giant egg timers in their middles – out of eight 'in play', by twisting them before their time runs out. Beforehand (supposedly), the contestant's accumulated jackpot is randomly hidden behind one of the twisters; after the final twist, the ones that were kept in play are revealed and the money is either behind one of them or one that's gone out of play… If all eight have been kept in play, of course, the contestant will win their jackpot (though the scenario is rarely seen due to the difficulty of the task); the cruelty of chance comes in that a player who saves seven twisters might still see their jackpot behind the eighth unsaved one, whereas a player who saves only one could find theirs there. Despite probability making these outcomes all the less likely, their risk is nonetheless a factor.

Other recent game-show productions have been similar; *Tipping Point* sees contestants playing a giant version of the 2p or 10p coin-pusher arcade games, ultimately putting their fate at the hands of the *tipping point*, rather than solely in their ability to answer the questions correctly; and probably most popularly and famously, *Deal or No Deal* relies fundamentally on the chance of guesswork and hope. The narrative of UK game/quiz shows seems then to have moved from the cerebral meritocratic model, through a teambuilding paradigm (*The Weakest Link*, for example), to greed-based deadlocks (e.g. ITV's *Golden Balls*, in which who wins money at the end is determined by two contestants choosing in secret between 'split' or 'steal'; i.e. two 'splits' divides the pot between them, one 'steal' and one 'split' gives the entire pot to the stealer, and two 'steals' equals two losers), and, finally, to cruel determinations made by chance.

We may wonder where this narratological shift in modern play comes from, and it might not be amiss to trace in its stages a mirroring of the capitalistic states of modern work. Such work is typified by the zero-hour contract, the sending of endless applications into the abyss of nonresponse, and, ultimately, the acceptance of the fact (ideologically told/sold to us) that we are subject to the whim of market and economic crises – beyond employers' control – that dictate the state of our employability, job security and benefit entitlement. Work-based traits are everywhere in modern play: from free-market-economy notions of the best candidates winning, through neoliberal business jargon that goes with the ubiquitous 'teambuilding exercise', and individualistic greed-mongering in the stock-market economy, to these precarious positions.

As alluded to above, the modern proletariat is known now as the 'precariat' (representative of temps and zero-hourers in a state of constant precarity in relation to the job market); luck – over skills and qualifications – now increasingly defines the chances of employment; and the ability to save for the future and meet the financial demands of the present is becoming increasingly difficult. These hallmarks of modern work are reappearing in modern play (even the last, in console gaming; the simple parables of Mario collecting coins, and Sonic rings, seem no longer as prevalent). In *Of Grammatology*, Jacques Derrida states: 'all that desire had wished to wrest from the play of language finds itself recaptured within that play'; perhaps it is that the surpluses of the games played in today's working world find themselves ideologically recaptured in its modern play too.[111]

Only Readers Left in Love? Reading Class in Classing Reading

According to an *Elite Daily* dating-advice article entitled 'Why Readers, Scientifically, are the Best People to Fall in Love With', 'finding someone who reads is like dating a thousand souls':

It's gaining the experience they've gained from everything

they've ever read and the wisdom that comes with those experiences. It's like dating a professor, a romantic and an explorer. If you date someone who reads, then you, too, will live a thousand different lives.[112]

One of the cognitive-psychology reports loosely cited to bolster this assertion aims to distinguish between the effects of reading fiction and non-fiction on the social empathy and 'real-world' capabilities of readers solely of either, whereas the above article – which has had over a million likes and shares – has ditched this distinction (in its obvious presumption that fiction is the only type of book) and claims that 'better people' are those that read.[113] Yet, if read closely, the standpoint of the article actually reveals itself as selfishly proclaiming that a better lover for you awaits in the form of the apparently woefully diminishing reader, from whom you'll be able to absorb all their acquired wisdom, whether you yourself are a reader or not.

What the article and the psychology behind it nonetheless do in common is *pathologise* reading; that is, make it the underlying cause of certain symptoms, be they 'positive' (the claim that social adjustment comes from reading fiction), or 'negative' (the claim that reading non-fiction is in fact more likely to lead to social awkwardness), or hyperbolic (the claims of the article concerning readers making the best lovers, even the best people in general). The problem with these claims seems to lie in the causal ordering of the research; in one of the scientific reports, reading is often construed as 'print-exposure' to the 'genres' of fiction and non-fiction. The research in fact sets out by subtracting readers' very subjectivity and substituting reader-types (the fiction reader/the non-fiction reader) for types of reading (the agency of selecting a text, of combining it with and setting it off against other texts; practices of literary theory and criticism, and the assumption of these into other disciplines). It also takes no account of types of writing (there appears to be no place for poetry, for example, nor for textual practices that blur the lines between fiction and non-fiction, from gonzo journalism to deconstruction) nor of the history of literature (the novel, for example, is in fact a relatively novel form of literature; there is no room made for the fact that reading itself, and the reasons for it, might have changed over the course of time, if those reasons have ever been homogeneous, that is).

The question of the research's *gaze* is also crucial here, and left out of its rationale: the goal that it and the article set out after, 'empathy', is in fact their point of departure; it is not their objective experimental result, but rather the result they have *desired*. They posit empathy as the best of all possible outcomes of reading, leading to the conclusion in the article that 'those who read fiction are capable of the most empathy and "theory of mind," which is the ability to hold opinions, beliefs and interests apart from their own'.[114] But this obsession with empathy has particular effects when superimposed upon a particular type of reading, such as Marxism, and its ideological underpinnings begin to show through. According to this 'reading = empathic-lovers' principle it would seem Marxist readers would have to disavow the discourse's tenets and advocate a 'love thy exploiter' policy in accord with their ability to 'entertain other ideas, without rejecting them and still retain their own'.[115] Otherwise, this principle could only set out to expose Marxism as perverted or propagandist, due to its transgression of the 'empathic reader-lover' principle. But, when these foundations are revealed, this might then rather show the 'empathic-reader' principle's own position as propaganda.

Thus, what the scientificity of the psychological research and the hierarchical classifying of the *Elite Daily* article in fact achieve is only caricaturing readers and reading. Despite their intentions perhaps, the old distinctions between the sciences and the humanities nevertheless are playing themselves out in these theatres of the psychological laboratory and the populist blog.

Reading's here become hijacked as the domain of scientific scrutiny; reading's function is made out to be the facilitation of love and wellbeing (which seems only a few steps away from it being characterised as 'overly sensitive' or aloofly 'effete', as humanities departments have so often been regarded by those of the harder sciences), the flipside of which is that its own efficaciousness in terms of social and political impact becomes diminished; and finally – in further banging the nail into this coffin – through this, reading's place in social discourse is only further dismantled, as state funding and support of the humanities dwindles. We must thus guard against study by reading becoming as Margaret Thatcher once labelled that of ancient Norse literature: 'a luxury'.[116] Indeed, reading must always remain more than a privilege and amusement of the elite.

a)

What is thus called for, needed, for the wilderness years that lie ahead, in the UK especially – in which we must remember that the Left remains only 'in opposition' to a government fully under the control of the Conservative Party – is a radically *democratic* reading. We hope that this is what this book partakes of, and we further envisage beginning to arise such phenomena as what Lacan called 'cartels'; that is, small reading groups designed to go over texts (and what isn't a text?) with fine toothcombs, for the purposes of facilitating productive responses and opening up possibilities. Indeed, as Mark Fisher has stated:

Of particular importance, it seems to me, is a popular demystification of economics and "the economy". The austerity myth has only seemed credible because of a widespread economic illiteracy – an illiteracy I very much share. Economics functions now much as theology functioned in the medieval world – as an intricate and elaborate system of concepts, objects and reasoning that is closed to non-initiates. We need something like a Reformation in and against capitalist economics – the equivalent of the Bible being translated into English. I think this could be done, not by a series of large-scale conferences, television [programmes], or films – although of course these wouldn't hurt – but virally. Small groups of people, including at least one individual who is an expert in economics, could get together and talk through some key concepts and principles, major economic events, etc. This could take place in private homes, in universities and colleges, in social clubs. […] In addition to everything else, this would also serve the function of reviving sociality, of re-building a class consciousness that has been dissipated by the individualising tendencies of neoliberalism and communicative capitalism.[117]

As much as our efforts are required, this highlights that it is also the reading materials themselves that need to be surrendered up by that class – that *elite* – which guards them so scrupulously under the proviso: 'whatever its popularity, *we* know what we're doing; leave it to us, the experts, the professionals'. It is these materials that we need to apprehend and read scrutinously, for – as Hunter S. Thompson said – 'when the going gets weird, the weird turn pro'.

7

Afterword

We want to leave the discussion open, and so this is a book without a traditional 'conclusion'. In its place, these are a few final remarks by the editors reflecting on the experience of editing the book and of working on the project of Everyday Analysis in general. As a collective group, of many contributors who are included in this volume and a great many more people working with and around us outside of these pages, we believe that more (and more diverse) political discussion is not only needed but is (thankfully) unavoidably coming. With that in mind, we have tried to present this book as a 'conversation', offering a variety of separate but interrelated pieces with various responses (in the form of agreements, extensions and oppositions) to them throughout, with the goal of going some way beyond the mere diagnostic manual, into something 'politactical'. And the conversation, we hope, will long go on. A great many people were invited to respond to the articles here, and none of those responses were ignored. We welcome any further responses to this book and are always looking for new contributors; the details for getting in contact are on our website, where we urge all readers to go if they want to join us or discuss our work.

As editors trying to create a platform for effective left-wing discussion with at least some ambition to help create political change (no matter how slow and slight), we have encountered many problems, resistances and stumbling blocks in the relatively short three years since the birth of Everyday Analysis. Some of these are unavoidable: funding issues, time constraints, logistical issues and the like. Other problems take a time to overcome: the slowly growing reach of articles, the battle to overcome resistance from more mainstream and right-wing media outlets whom we often need the help of to expand our platform and reach but must resist becoming a part of, for example. Others still we have already begun to work against, and we would like to make a particular call to arms for continued collectivity. Newsfeeds are full of petty leftist *ressentiment*, and our posts have sometimes received dismissals from those working very closely to our own project. Sometimes a meme is used to point out the article is nothing more than an idea that is already circulating. Sometimes articles are dismissed for being too popular, sometimes too political, sometimes too theoretical. Very rarely are these dismissals coming from the Right, but from the Left, from people (broadly speaking) committed to similar political agendas to our own. Likewise, our academic experience, for example, has shown us how radical political Derrideans can dedicate large amounts of time and effort to the dismissal of radical political Lacanians, and vice versa. Talking of *ressentiment*, Friedrich Nietzsche writes:

That lambs dislike great birds of prey does not seem strange: only it gives no ground for reproaching these birds of prey for bearing off little lambs. And if the lambs say among themselves: 'these birds of prey are evil; and whoever is least like a bird of prey, but rather its opposite, a Lamb—would he not be good?'[118]

It is not so much a question of thinking of the radical as a bird of prey or as a lamb, but of seeing how the reproach of the other establishes a feeling of morality-like 'good' in the reproacher. This leads to Nietzschean *ressentiment*, in which frustrations that should be directed at those in power are instead directed to one's nearest colleagues and neighbours. This is something we are increasingly seeing in left-wing circles, and it is dividing and separating us, preventing political action and collectivity. Whilst individuals might feel 'good' compared to the others they reproach, what is missing is a sense of working together and directing our anger to the right targets. Indeed, as Russell Brand (one often so pilloried) put it in his *New Statesman* editorial: 'it's been said that: "The right seeks converts and the left seeks traitors." This moral superiority that is peculiar to the Left is a great impediment to momentum.'[119] If Everyday Analysis can modestly claim to have achieved anything at all thus far, it is in working against this *ressentiment* and encouraging collective action among diverse individuals. In this sense, we need not agree with each other in order to work together. The conversational approach in this book has been an attempt to show this, working towards political action without requiring those involved to subscribe to the same strict agenda.

8

Notes

1. See Mark Fisher, *Capitalist Realism: Is There No Alternative?* (Winchester: O-Books, 2009).
2. See also EDA Collective, 'A Politics Now!', in *Twerking to Turking: Everyday Analysis, Volume 2* (Winchester: Zero Books, 2015) pp.202-205.
3. See, for example, Jack Sommers, 'Owen Jones Asked To Stand As MP Against Nick Clegg, He Tells Huffington Post UK', http://www.huffingtonpost.co.uk/2014/09/10/owen-jones-mehdi-hasan-conversation_n_5799294.html?utm_hp_ref=mostpopular, and Anonymous, 'Owen Jones Refuses To Rule Out Running As MP', http://www.lbc.co.uk/owen-jones-refuses-to-rule-out-running-as-mp-114749
4. Theodor Adorno, *Minima Moralia: Reflections from Damaged Life*, trans. by E. F. N. Jephcott (London: Verso Radical Thinkers, 2005) pp.69-70.
5. See Dan Bloom, 'Petition for BBC to call David Cameron "right-wing Prime Minister" backed by 65,000 people', http://www.mirror.co.uk/news/uk-news/petition-bbc-call-david-cameron-6462386, and the petition itself at: https://www.change.org/p/bbc-request-for-the-bbc-to-refer-to-david-cameron-as-the-right-wing-prime-minister
6. Gilles Deleuze, *Proust and Signs: The Complete Text*, trans. by Richard Howard (London: Continuum, 2008) pp.72-73.
7. Charles Baudelaire, *My Heart Laid Bare and Other Prose Writings*, ed. by Peter Quennell, trans. by Norman Cameron (New York: Haskell House, 1975) p.156.
8. Walter Benjamin, *The Arcades Project*, ed. by Rolf Tiedemann, trans. by Howard Eiland and Kevin McLaughlin

(Cambridge, MA: The Belknap Press of Harvard University Press, 1999) p.61.

9. See Alex Andreou, 'Anti-homeless spikes: "Sleeping rough opened my eyes to the city's barbed cruelty"', http://www.theguardian.com/society/2015/feb/18/defensive-architecture-keeps-poverty-undeen-and-makes-us-more-hostile

10. See also EDA Collective, '*Poversion*: The Perverse Position of Poverty Porn' and 'Amazon Turk and Inevitable Capitalism', in *Twerking to Turking*, pp.102-104 and pp.239-241.

11. Sam Tonkin, 'Gary Neville drops in to meet the squatters who have moved into the hotel he owns with Ryan Giggs after agreeing to let them stay for the winter', http://www.dailymail.co.uk/news/article-3291418/Gary-Neville-drops-meet-squatters-moved-hotel-owns-Ryan-Giggs-agreeing-let-stay-winter.html

12. 'Northern Stock Exchange: List Entry Summary', http://www.historicengland.org.uk/listing/the-list/list-entry/1271383

13. See Matt Lawton, 'Malky Mackay apologises for "friendly text message banter" over racism claim... but denies sexist and homophobic slurs', http://www.dailymail.co.uk/sport/football/article-2731139/Malky-Mackay-apologies-friendly-text-banter-former-Cardiff-boss-reported-FA.html

14. See EDA Collective, 'The Politics of the Man Booker Prize', http://www.everydayanalysis.com/post/100070534629/the-politics-of-the-man-booker-prize0

15. See Jacques Rancière, 'Ten Theses on Politics', *Theory & Event*, vol. 5, no. 3 (2001). Available here: http://www.egs.edu/faculty/jacques-ranciere/articles/ten-thesis-on-politics/

16. See Sianne Ngai, *Ugly Feelings* (Cambridge, MA: Harvard University Press, 2005) p.4.

17. Jacques Lacan, *The Seminar of Jacques Lacan, Book I: Freud's Papers on Technique, 1953-1954*, ed. by Jacques-Alain Miller,

trans. by John Forrester (New York: W. W. Norton, 1988) p.167.

18. For the event, see Anonymous, 'What next in Tottenham?', http://www.socialistworker.co.uk/art.php?id=25741

19. See Max Ehrenfreund, 'What we know about what happened in Ferguson', http://www.washingtonpost.com /news/wonkblog/wp/2014/11/25/get-completely-caught-up-on-whats-happened-in-ferguson/, EDA Collective, 'The Mark Duggan Inquest: *Politicians and Fetishistic Disavowal'*, and Matt Wells and Simon Jeffery, 'UK riots aftermath – Friday 12 August 2011', http://www.theguardian.com/uk /blog/2011/aug/12/uk-riots-day-six-aftermath#block-39

20. See Jane Onyanga-Omara and John Bacon, 'Police: Video clearly shows shooting of Ohio boy, 12', http://www. usatoday.com/story/news/nation/2014/11/24/cleveland-shot-boy/19471925/

21. See Keir Mudie and Mark Conrad, 'I watched Tory MP MURDER a boy during depraved Westminster VIP paedophile party', http://www.mirror.co.uk/news/uk-news /i-watched-tory-mp-murder-4636497 and Ben Riley-Smith, 'Historic Westminster child abuse and murder claims "only tip of the iceberg" in scandal, Theresa May warns', http:// www.telegraph.co.uk/news/uknews/law-and-order/112 48683/Historic-Westminster-child-abuse-and-murder-claims-only-tip-of-the-iceberg-in-scandal-Theresa-May-warns.html

22. See Daniel Boffey, 'Edwardian house at heart of a long-simmering sex scandal', http://www.theguardian.com /politics/2014/jul/05/elm-guest-house-paedophile-network-allegations; Iain Watson, 'Butler-Sloss steps down from child abuse inquiry', http://www.bbc.co.uk/news/business-28295282; Rowena Mason, 'Fiona Woolf resigns as chair of government's child abuse inquiry', http://www.theguardian .com/politics/2014/oct/31/fiona-woolf-resigns-chairman-

child-abuse-inquiry; Alan Travis, 'Theresa May avoids questions over Wanless review on missing files', http://www.theguardian.com/politics/2014/nov/11/theresa-may-wanless-review-dickens-dossier; and Daily Mail Reporter, 'Murdered Crimewatch presenter Jill Dando "tried to get bosses to investigate alleged paeodphile [sic] ring inside the BBC but no one wanted to know"', http://www.dailymail.co.uk/news/article-2698820/Murd ered-Crimewatch-presenter-Jill-Dando-tried-bosses-inves-tigate-alleged-paeodphile-ring-inside-BBC-no-one-wanted-know.html

23. Josh Halliday, 'Father claims police covered up son's murder by Westminster paedophile ring', http://www.the guardian.com/society/2014/nov/19/father-police-covered-up-sons-murder-westminster-paedophile-ring

24. See 'Six degrees of separation', Wikipedia, 'https://en.wiki pedia.org/wiki/Six_degrees_of_separation

25. See Myles Jackman, 'THE FOLLOWING CONTENT IS NOT ACCEPTABLE', http://mylesjackman.com/index.php/my-blog/106-the-following-content-is-not-acceptable

26. See Frankie Mullen, 'British BDSM Enthusiasts, Say Goodbye to Your Favourite Homegrown Porn', http://www.vice.com/en_uk/read/the-end-of-uk-bdsm-282; Pandora Blake, 'Online porn: the canary in the coalmine', http://pandorablake.com/blog/2014/12/canary-coalmine-online-porn-atvod; and Erika Lust, 'The new UK porn legislation will turn erotic film into boring, unrealistic male fantasy', http://www.independent.co.uk/voices/comment/the-new-uk-porn-legislation-will-turn-erotic-film-into-boring-unrealistic-male-fantasy-9898052.html

27. Michel Foucault, The Will to Knowledge: The History of Sexuality, Volume 1, trans. by Robert Hurley (London: Penguin Books, 1998) p.11.

28. Roland Barthes, A Lover's Discourse: Fragments, trans. by

Richard Howard (New York: Hill and Wang, 1978) p.137. Bataille states: 'we are admitted to the knowledge of a pleasure in which the notion of pleasure is mingled with mystery, suggestive of the taboo that fashions the pleasure at the same time as it condemns it'. See Georges Bataille, *Eroticism: Death and Sensuality*, trans. by Mary Dalwood (London: Marion Boyars, 2006) p.107.

29. See Christopher Hooton, 'A long list of sex acts just got banned in UK porn', http://www.independent.co.uk/news/uk/a-long-list-of-sex-acts-just-got-banned-in-uk-porn-9897174.html

30. Robin Bauer, *Queer BDSM Intimacies: Critical Consent and Pushing Boundaries* (Basingstoke: Palgrave Macmillan, 2014) p.245.

31. Ibid. p.246.

32. Quoted in ibid. p.234.

33. See Inigo Thomas, 'Gove's Enemies of Promise', http://www.lrb.co.uk/blog/2013/03/25/inigo-thomas/goves-enemies-of-promise/

34. Department for Education, 'Transparency data: Open academies and academy projects in development', https://www.gov.uk/government/publications/open-academies-and-academy-projects-in-development

35. Department for Education, 'Transparency data: Free schools: open schools and successful applications', https://www.gov.uk/government/publications/free-schools-open-schools-and-successful-applications

36. See Department for Education and The Rt Hon Lord Hill of Oareford CBE, 'Academies to have same freedom as free schools over teachers', https://www.gov.uk/government/news/academies-to-have-same-freedom-as-free-schools-over-teachers

37. The Office for Standards in Education, Children's Services and Skills (Ofsted), 'Raising Standards, Improving Lives:

The Office for Standards in Education, Children's Services and Skills (Ofsted) Strategic Plan 2014 to 2016', https://www.gov.uk/government/uploads/system/uploads/attachment_data/file/379920/Ofsted_20Strategic_20Plan_20 2014-16.pdf

38. Department for Business, Innovation and Skills, 'Fulfilling our Potential: Teaching Excellence, Social Mobility and Student Choice', https://www.gov.uk/government/uploads /system/uploads/attachment_data/file/474266/BIS-15-623-fulfilling-our-potential-teaching-excellence-social-mobility-and-student-choice-accessible.pdf (p.12).

39. Theodor Adorno, 'The Jargon of Authenticity', trans. by Rodney Livingstone, in *Can One Live After Auschwitz? A Philosophical Reader*, ed. by Rolf Tiedemann (Stanford: Stanford University Press, 2003) p.166.

40. See Kashmira Gander, 'Conservative Party conference: David Cameron accidentally says Tories "resent" the poor', http://www.independent.co.uk/news/uk/politics/conservative-party-conference-david-cameron-accidentally-says-tories-resent-the-poor-9768106.html

41. Alenka Zupančič, *The Odd One In: On Comedy* (Cambridge, Mass: MIT Press, 2008), p.34.

42. **b)** To respond to the points being made in this response, the old distinction between perversity and perversion might come back into play here, the former referring to a vice-like practice, willfully carried out, indeed, perhaps by the morally deranged, and the latter to a psychopathological manifestation, often involved in a repetition compulsion. It is clearly the first of these that is that of the initiation ceremony, the once-performed proof that one is up to the test in the show of willing in response to peer pressure, and thus an act that is more *perverse* than it is perverted. On similar issues as the abovementioned, see Everyday Analysis, 'Fort/LAD, or, LAD Beyond the Pleasure

Principle', http://www.everydayanalysis.com/post/46607928
766/fortlad-or-lad-beyond-the-pleasure-principle

43. Russell Brand and Ed Miliband, 'Milibrand: The Interview -
    OFFICIAL VIDEO The Trews (E309)', https://www.youtube
    .com/watch?v=RDZm9_uKtyo&list=PL5BY9veyhGt46KMm
    gAJYi1LF0EUkpqcrX&index=1; and Media Mole, 'David
    Cameron has no "time to hang out with Russell Brand" – but
    fits Jeremy Clarkson and Katie Hopkins in', http://www.
    newstatesman.com/media-mole/2015/04/david-cameron-
    has-no-time-hang-out-russell-brand-fits-jeremy-clarkson-
    and-katie

44. See Prospect Team, 'World thinkers 2015: the results',
    http://www.prospectmagazine.co.uk/world/world-thinkers-
    2015-the-results-thomas-piketty-russell-brand-revolution;
    The Trews; and *The Emperor's New Clothes*, dir. by Michael
    Winterbottom, 2015.

45. See, for example, Patrick Wintour, 'Ed Miliband spotted
    leaving Russell Brand's London home', http://www.the
    guardian.com/politics/2015/apr/28/ed-miliband-spotted-
    leaving-russell-brand-london-home

46. Mark Fisher, 'Limbo is Over – kpunk election post #1',
    http://repeaterbooks.com/2015/04/27/limbo-is-over-new-
    kpunk-post/. See also Fisher, *Capitalist Realism*.

47. See Jacques Lacan, 'The Subversion of the Subject and the
    Dialectic of Desire in the Freudian Unconscious', in *Écrits:
    The First Complete Edition in English*, trans. by Bruce Fink, in
    collaboration with Héloïse Fink and Russell Grigg (New
    York: W. W. Norton, 2006) p.688.

48. Anonymous, 'John McDonnell: Chairman Mao quotes were
    "a joke"', http://www.bbc.co.uk/news/uk-politics-34931047

49. See, for example, Media Mole, 'John McDonnell's Mao
    zinger spectacularly backfires', http://www.newstatesman
    .com/politics/economy/2015/11/john-mcdonnells-mao-
    zinger-spectacularly-backfires

50. Available at http://www.lbc.co.uk/damian-mcbride-id-shoot-whoever-suggested-mao-stunt-120406

51. See EDA Collective, 'The Scrabble Squabble; or, the Plight of Online Opposition', in *Twerking to Turking*, pp.235-236.

52. Honour Bayes, 'We're surprised by the election result because our view is too narrow', https://www.thestage .co.uk/opinion/2015/honour-bayes-surprised-election-result-view-narrow/

53. See Jane Martinson, 'Scottish Sun backs the SNP: is Rupert Murdoch pulling the strings?', http://www.theguardian .com/media/2015/apr/30/scottish-sun-snp-rupert-murdoch-nicola-sturgeon

54. With the return of a leftist politics in Labour, the concept of the 'Centre-Left' has had to come to the realisation that it must weigh itself in relation not only to the political spectrum as a whole, but in relation to its party's politics. To put it diagrammatically, we see:
On the political spectrum:

('Centre-Left')
Left_____Centre_____Right

On the Labour spectrum:

('Centre-Left', i.e. right)
Left (the left wing)_____Centre (the right wing)

That is, if political thinking on the Left cannot go any further than the Centre without becoming a rightist thinking (and necessitating defection to another party), proximity to that Centre represents the pull to, and sliding towards, the Right (this proximity can then be used as an apparatus to measure the party's fidelity to its politics). The Liberal Democrats' failure as a party is representative of the pitfalls of this grey, non-committal area. Thus, a real Centre-Left can only be locatable here:

(Centre-Left)
Left_____Centre_____Right

and the proper designation of the former 'Centre-Left' as the 'Right-Left' highlights its own paradox and oxymoron.

55. Jeremy Corbyn, quoted in Rowena Mason and Frances Perraudin, 'Jeremy Corbyn: Labour membership will determine policy, not me', http://www.theguardian .com/pol itics/2015/aug/27/jeremy-corbyn-labour-membership-policy-leadership

56. See Jon Stone, 'Jeremy Corbyn creates new dedicated "Minister for Mental Health" in his shadow cabinet', http://www.independent.co.uk/news/uk/politics/jeremy-corbyn-creates-new-dedicated-minister-for-mental-health-in-his-shadow-cabinet-10500075.html

57. James Curran, 'Introduction', in *The Future of the Left*, ed. by James Curran (Cambridge: Polity Press & New Socialist, 1984) p.x.

58. Edith Hancock, 'Corbyn is not the first to pitch a quantitative easing for people', http://www.cityam.com/224 630/strange-bedfellows-corbyn-not-first-pitch-people-s-qe

59. See Owen Jones, *Chavs: The Demonization of the Working Class* (London: Verso, 2011) p.252.

60. Ernesto Laclau, 'Structure, History and the Political', in Judith Butler, Ernesto Laclau and Slavoj Žižek, *Contingency, Hegemony, Universality: Contemporary Dialogues on the Left* (London: Verso, 2000) p.211.

61. See Dominic Sandbrook, 'Labour's greatest leaders were patriots and monarchists. Today, they'd be spinning in their graves', http://www.dailymail.co.uk/debate/article-32377 34/DOMINIC-SANDBROOK-Labour-s-greatest-leaders-

patriots-monarchists-Today-d-spinning-graves.html; Harry Cole and Stephen Moyes, 'Court Jezter: Leftie who hates the royals WILL kiss Queen's hand to grab £6.2m', http://www.thesun.co.uk/sol/homepage/news/politics/6639 537/Jeremy-Corbyn-to-kiss-the-Queens-hand.html; and Phil Harrison, 'Fangs Bared: On Jeremy Corbyn & Media Treatment, http://thequietus.com/articles/18790-jeremy-corbyn-media-treatment-battle-of-britain. 'Even if you can't sing, you should stand there mouthing the words', Jenni Russell said on *Newsnight*.

62. On Obama and the Pledge of Allegiance, see Bill Adair, 'Photo was taken during anthem, not pledge', http://www.politifact.com/truth-o-meter/statements/2007/nov/08/chain-email/photo-was-taken-during-anthem-not-pledge/

63. See, for example, Georgina Stubbs, 'Who is Jeremy Corbyn? This is Everything You Need to Know', http://www.sunnation.co.uk/who-is-jeremy-corbyn-this-is-everything-you-need-to-know/

64. See Andy Burnham, 'A Radical Labour Vision for the 21st Century', http://www.labour.org.uk/blog/entry/a-radical-labour-vision-for-the-21st-century; Yvette Cooper, 'I will deliver a radical – and credible – Labour alternative to Tory austerity', http://www.theguardian.com/commentisfree/2015/aug/23/my-radical-labour-alternative-tory-austerity-corbyn-print-money-deficit; and Jon Stone, 'Liz Kendall says she is "the real anti-austerity candidate" for Labour leader', http://www.independent.co.uk/news/uk/politics/liz-kendall-says-she-is-the-real-anti-austerity-candidate-for-labour-leader-10481346.html

65. See, for example, Andrew Gilligan, 'Jeremy Corbyn, friend to Hamas, Iran and extremists', http://www.telegraph.co.uk/news/politics/labour/11749043/Andrew-Gilligan-Jeremy-Corbyn-friend-to-Hamas-Iran-and-extremists.html

66. On this, see Julian Baggini, 'Jeremy Corbyn's first move as leader? Remove the Labour whip', http://www.theguardian.com/commentisfree/2015/aug/31/jeremy-corbyn-leader-remove-labour-whip

67. For the line on the bicycle, see Dominic Kennedy and Sam Coates, 'Marr is snubbed for a day at church', http://www.thetimes.co.uk/tto/news/politics/article4556099.ece

68. See, for example, Polly Toynbee, 'In Labour's leadership race, Yvette Cooper is the one to beat', http://www.theguardian.com/commentisfree/2015/jun/23/labour-leadership-race-yvette-cooper-andy-burnham

69. See Peter Hain, 'Jeremy Corbyn's policies may be popular – but they don't add up to a platform', http://www.theguardian.com/commentisfree/2015/jul/30/jeremy-corbyn-policies-labour

70. See https://www.barackobama.com/

71. http://www.medialens.org/; https://www.facebook.com/corbynmedia?fref=ts; and https://www.facebook.com/groups/MediaVsCorbyn/?fref=ts#_=_

72. See Owen Jones, 'If Jeremy Corbyn's Labour is going to work, it has to communicate', http://www.theguardian.com/commentisfree/2015/sep/16/jeremy-corbyn-labour-twitter-media

73. For this, see the short video of John McDonnell's talk 'Riots, Recession & Resistance' (11 August 2011) available at https://www.youtube.com/watch?v=PM-p-ZZVkYo

74. Guy Debord, Comments on the Society of the Spectacle, trans. by Malcolm Imrie (London: Verso, 1998), p.48.

75. See Slavoj Žižek, 'Eastern European liberalism and its discontents', in The Universal Exception, ed. by Rex Butler and Scott Stephens (London: Bloomsbury Academic, 2014) p.30.

76. Kunal Modi, 'Facebook status, 17 September 2014' sharing Tariq Ali, 'Scots, undo this union of rogues. Independence is

the only way to fulfil your potential', http://www.theguard
ian.com/commentisfree/2014/mar/13/scots-undo-union-of-
rogues-independence-1707-honour

77. See Jacques Rancière, *The Politics of Aesthetics: The
Distribution of the Sensible*, trans. by Gabriel Rockhill
(London: Continuum, 2004).

78. Slavoj Žižek, *Organs Without Bodies: On Deleuze and
Consequences* (Abingdon: Routledge Classics, 2012) p.85.
Also, see http://www.coxar.pwp.blueyonder.co.uk/ for the
parody HTTP 404 webpage that claimed 'these Weapons of
Mass Destruction cannot be displayed' in response to the
war on Iraq, and suggested: 'click the Bomb button if you
are Donald Rumsfeld'.

79. See Ross Hawkins, 'Jeremy Corbyn row after "I'd not fire
nuclear weapons" comment', http://www.bbc.co.uk/news
/uk-politics-34399565

80. See also EDA Collective, 'On Žižek Writing for the
Guardian', in *Twerking to Turking*, pp.174-176.

81. Daniel Ellsberg, quoted in Julian Assange, 'Introduction:
WikiLeaks and Empire', in *The WikiLeaks Files: The World
According to US Empire* (London: Verso, 2015) p.18.

82. Natalie Stone, 'Obama Offers Advice to Presidential
Hopeful Kanye West: "You Got to Deal With Strange
Characters"', http://www.hollywoodreporter.com/news
/obama-offers-advice-presidential-hopeful-831211

83. On this, see Maxwell Strachan, 'The Definitive History Of
"George Bush Doesn't Care About Black People"',
http://www.huffingtonpost.com/entry/kanye-west-george-
bush-black-people_55d67c12e4b020c386de2f5e

84. See Kirsten Acuna, 'Here's the full speech Kanye West gave
at the VMAs that everyone is talking about', http://
uk.businessinsider.com/kanye-west-mtv-vmas-speech-
2015-8

85. Chris Hedges, *Empire of Illusion: The End of Literacy and the*

Triumph of Spectacle (New York, Nation Books, 2010) p.190.

86. See, for example, Amanda Holpuch, 'Muslim woman ejected from Donald Trump rally after silent protest', http://www.theguardian.com/us-news/2016/jan/09/muslim-woman-ejected-donald-trump-rally-silent-protest and Tina Nguyen, 'Donald Trump's Rallies Are Becoming Increasingly Violent', http://www.vanityfair.com/news/2016/03/donald-trump-protesters-rally-violence

87. See Cheryl K. Chumley, "'No Muslim' signs at Texas shopping center spark ire', http://www.washingtontimes.com/news/2013/aug/9/texas-shopping-center-parking-signs-no-muslims/ and Ben Handelman, '"Just unbelievable:" Anti-Muslim note posted at grocery store shocks customers, store officials alike', http://fox6now.com/2015/12/08/just-unbelievable-anti-muslim-note-posted-at-grocery-store-shocks-customers-store-officials-alike/#

88. See Carl Schreck, 'A Filmmaker's Chilling View Of Russia's Antigay 'Vigilantes'', http://www.rferl.org/content/filmmaker-anti-gay-vigilantes-/26622840.html

89. See The Paperboy, http://www.thepaperboy.com/uk/2012/12/15/front-pages-archive.cfm

90. The Paperboy, http://www.thepaperboy.com/uk/2014/12/17/front-pages-archive.cfm

91. David Cameron, https://twitter.com/David_Cameron/status/279690130955059200

92. David Cameron, https://twitter.com/david_cameron/status/544786149525700608

93. See Anonymous, 'President Obama condemns "depraved" school terrorists', http://www.itv.com/news/update/2014-12-16/president-obama-condemns-depraved-school-terrorists/

94. See http://www.awaregirls.org, and Billy Briggs, 'The Peshawar women fighting the Taliban: "We cannot trust anyone"', http://www.theguardian.com/cities/2015/oct/13

/the-peshawar-women-fighting-the-taliban-we-cannot-trust-anyone

95. Frances Ryan, 'Why do we care more about Cecil the Lion than we do about the "swarm" of migrants at Calais?', http://www.newstatesman.com/politics/2015/07/why-do-care-more-about-cecil-lion-we-do-about-swarm-migrants-calais

96. See 'What Happens When Something Fascist Happens? What the Queen's Nazi Salute Shows Us', above.

97. Wills Robinson, 'Has a poacher killed Cecil's brother? Zimbabwe park claims ANOTHER lion has been shot dead - and it may be cub protector Jericho', http://www.dailymail.co.uk/news/article-3182428/Cecil-s-brother-Jericho-shot-dead-poachers-Zimbabwean-park.html; and Simon Tomlinson and Tom Wyke, 'Saved... for now: Cecil the lion's cubs are being protected by his BROTHER after fears rival male will kill them and take over the pride, says Oxford University expert', http://www.dailymail.co.uk/news/article-3181277/Saved-Cecil-lion-s-cubs-protected-BROTHER-fears-evil-rival-Jericho-kill-pride-says-Oxford-University-expert.html

98. Jacques Lacan, *The Seminar of Jacques Lacan, Book XIX: ...Ou pire/...Or worse, 1971-1972*, trans. by Cormac Gallagher (London: Karnac, unofficial translation, n.d.) session XII, p.12.

99. Paul Gilroy, 'Introduction: Race is Ordinary', in *There Ain't No Black in the Union Jack: The Cultural Politics of Race and Nation* (Abingdon: Routledge Classics, 2002) p.xxiv.

100. Ibid. p.xxv.

101. Ibid.

102. See Philip Kleinfeld, 'Calling Bullshit On the Anti-Refugee Memes Flooding the Internet', http://www.vice.com/en_uk/read/kleinfeld-refugee-memes-debunking-846

103. Frederick Douglass, *Narrative of the Life of Frederick Douglass,*

An American Slave, ed. by Houston A. Baker, Jr. (London: Penguin Classics, 1986) p.132.

104 Richard Klein, 'A Word on State Regulation of Psychoanalysis', http://declineatlittlea.blogspot.co.uk/

105. Ibid.

106. Gilroy, 'Introduction: Race is Ordinary', in *There Ain't No Black in the Union Jack*, p.xxv.

107. James O'Malley, 'Surprised that Syrian refugees have smartphones? Sorry to break this to you, but you're an idiot', http://www.independent.co.uk/voices/comment/surprised-that-syrian-refugees-have-smartphones-well-sorry-to-break-this-to-you-but-youre-an-idiot-10489719.html

108. On this phenomenon, see, for example, DarkSyde, 'Job seekers beware of the fake job postings', http://www.dailykos.com/story/2014/02/09/1274938/-Job-seekers-beware-of-the-fake-job-postings

109. Guy Standing, *The Precariat: The New Dangerous Class* (London: Bloomsbury Academic, 2011) pp.12-13.

110. See Andrew Grice, 'Tax credit cuts will encourage people to work as hard as the Chinese, says Jeremy Hunt', http://www.independent.co.uk/news/uk/politics/tax-credit-cuts-will-make-people-work-as-hard-as-the-chinese-says-jeremy-hunt-a6680836.html

111. Jacques Derrida, *Of Grammatology*, trans. by Gayatri Chakravorty Spivak (Baltimore: The Johns Hopkins University Press, 1997) corrected edn. p.6.

112. Lauren Martin, 'Why Readers, Scientifically, Are The Best People To Fall In Love With', http://elitedaily.com/life/culture/date-reader-readers-best-people-fall-love-scientifically-proven/662017/

113. See Raymond A. Mar, Keith Oatley, Jacob Hirsh, Jennifer dela Paz, Jordan B. Peterson, 'Bookworms versus nerds: Exposure to fiction versus non-fiction, divergent associations with social ability, and the simulation of fictional social

worlds', *Journal of Research in Personality*, vol. 40, no. 5 (October 2006), 694-712.

114. Martin, 'Why Readers, Scientifically, Are The Best People To Fall In Love With'.

115. Ibid.

116. See Stuart Lee, 'On university funding and the arts', https://www.youtube.com/watch?v=JDEZ2h41t0I, in which he recalls a piece of TV news in which Thatcher asked a girl at an Oxford college, 'What are you studying?', to which she replied, 'Ancient Norse Literature', garnering the riposte: 'Oh, what a luxury'.

117. Mark Fisher, 'Communist Realism – kpunk election post #2', http://repeaterbooks.com/2015/05/06/communist-realism-new-kpunk-election-post/

118. Friedrich Nietzsche, *On the Genealogy of Morals* and *Ecce Homo*, trans. by Walter Kaufmann (New York: Vintage, 1989) pp.44-45.

119. Russell Brand, 'We No Longer Have the Luxury of Tradition', *New Statesman*, October 2013.

Zero Books

CULTURE, SOCIETY & POLITICS

Contemporary culture has eliminated the concept and public figure of the intellectual. A cretinous anti-intellectualism presides, cheer-led by hacks in the pay of multinational corporations who reassure their bored readers that there is no need to rouse themselves from their stupor. Zer0 Books knows that another kind of discourse - intellectual without being academic, popular without being populist - is not only possible: it is already flourishing. Zer0 is convinced that in the unthinking, blandly consensual culture in which we live, critical and engaged theoretical reflection is more important than ever before.

If you have enjoyed this book, why not tell other readers by posting a review on your preferred book site. Recent bestsellers from Zero Books are:

In the Dust of This Planet
Horror of Philosophy vol. 1
Eugene Thacker
In the first of a series of three books on the Horror of Philosophy, In the Dust of This Planet offers the genre of horror as a way of thinking about the unthinkable.
Paperback: 978-1-84694-676-9 ebook: 978-1-78099-010-1

Capitalist Realism
Is there no alternative?
Mark Fisher
An analysis of the ways in which capitalism has presented itself
as the only realistic political-economic system.
Paperback: 978-1-84694-317-1 ebook: 978-1-78099-734-6

Rebel Rebel
Chris O'Leary
David Bowie: every single song. Everything you want to know,
everything you didn't know.
Paperback: 978-1-78099-244-0 ebook: 978-1-78099-713-1

Cartographies of the Absolute
Alberto Toscano, Jeff Kinkle
An aesthetics of the economy for the twenty-first century.
Paperback: 978-1-78099-275-4 ebook: 978-1-78279-973-3

Malign Velocities
Accelerationism and Capitalism
Benjamin Noys
Long listed for the Bread and Roses Prize 2015, Malign
Velocities argues against the need for speed, tracking acceler-
ation as the symptom of the on-going crises of capitalism.
Paperback: 978-1-78279-300-7 ebook: 978-1-78279-299-4

Meat Market
Female flesh under Capitalism
Laurie Penny
A feminist dissection of women's bodies as the fleshy fulcrum
of capitalist cannibalism, whereby women are both consumers
and consumed.
Paperback: 978-1-84694-521-2 ebook: 978-1-84694-782-7

Poor but Sexy
Culture Clashes in Europe East and West
Agata Pyzik
How the East stayed East and the West stayed West.
Paperback: 978-1-78099-394-2 ebook: 978-1-78099-395-9

Romeo and Juliet in Palestine
Teaching Under Occupation
Tom Sperlinger
Life in the West Bank, the nature of pedagogy and the role of a
university under occupation.
Paperback: 978-1-78279-637-4 ebook: 978-1-78279-636-7

Sweetening the Pill
or How we Got Hooked on Hormonal Birth Control
Holly Grigg-Spall
Has contraception liberated or oppressed women? Sweetening
the Pill breaks the silence on the dark side of hormonal contraception.
Paperback: 978-1-78099-607-3 ebook: 978-1-78099-608-0

**Readers of ebooks can buy or view any of these
bestsellers by clicking on the live link in the title. Most
titles are published in paperback and as an ebook.
Paperbacks are available in traditional bookshops. Both
print and ebook formats are available online.**

**Find more titles and sign up to our readers' newsletter at
http://www.johnhuntpublishing.com/culture-and-politics.
Follow us on Facebook at
https://www.facebook.com/ZeroBooks
and Twitter at https://twitter.com/Zer0Books.**